DECEMBER 1995

Sunday	Monday	Tuesday	Wednesday	Thursday	Friday	Saturday
					1	2
3	4	5	6	7	8	9
10	11	12	13	14	15	16
17	18	19	20	21	22	23
24 Christmas Eve	25 Christmas Day	26	27	28	29	30
31 New Year's Eve						

In the years to come, you'll be glad you noted the special times of the season on these pages.

Christmas

with Southern Living
1995

Oxmoor House®

Christmas
with Southern Living
1995

Edited by Rebecca Brennan,
Lelia Gray Neil, and Julie Fisher

©1995 by Oxmoor House, Inc.
Book Division of Southern Progress Corporation
P.O. Box 2463, Birmingham, Alabama 35201

Southern Living® is a federally registered trademark belonging to
Southern Living, Inc.

Library of Congress Catalog Card Number: 84-63032
ISBN: 0-8487-1445-8
ISSN: 0747-7791
Manufactured in the United States of America
First Printing

Editor-in-Chief: Nancy J. Fitzpatrick
Senior Homes Editor: Mary Kay Culpepper
Senior Foods Editor: Susan Carlisle Payne
Senior Editor, Editorial Services: Olivia Kindig Wells
Art Director: James Boone

Christmas with Southern Living 1995

Editor: Rebecca Brennan
Projects Editor: Lelia Gray Neil
Foods Editor: Julie Fisher
Assistant Art Director: Cynthia R. Cooper
Editorial Assistant: Adrienne E. Short
Copy Editors: L. Amanda Owens, Cecilia C. Matthews
Senior Photographers: Jim Bathie, John O'Hagan
Senior Photo Stylists: Kay E. Clarke, Katie Stoddard
Director, Test Kitchens: Kathleen Royal Phillips
Assistant Director, Test Kitchens: Gayle Hays Sadler
Test Kitchens Home Economists: Susan Hall Bellows, Julie Christopher, Iris Crawley,
    Michele Brown Fuller, Natalie E. King, Elizabeth Tyler Luckett, Jan A. Smith
Artist: Kelly Davis
Production and Distribution Director: Phillip Lee
Production Manager: Gail H. Morris
Associate Production Manager: Theresa L. Beste
Production Assistant: Marianne Jordan
Senior Production Designer: Larry Hunter
Publishing Systems Administrator: Rick Tucker

Front cover, top: Jeweled Cheesecake, page 19; bottom: Hot Fudge Cheesecake, page 20.
Back cover, top: Star Ornament, page 69; center: Rose Garland, page 55; bottom: Toile Stockings, page 48.

CONTENTS

THERE'S NO PLACE LIKE HOME

The *Southern Living* Idea House at Opryland brims with beautiful holiday decorations for you to make and your family to love.

Come in to a House Full of Holiday Cheer

The *Southern Living* Idea House is just steps away from Nashville's Grand Ole Opry. Starting with the beribboned cedar garlands on the front porch, every holiday idea in its rooms is simple, fast, and Christmassy.

At the table, each guest's place is marked with an innovative **party favor**. Simply write your guests' names on Christmas balls using a gold permanent paint pen. Remove the metal hook from the top of each ornament and fill the ornaments with water. Place flowers in the ornaments (here, a white Casablanca lily and a red rose) and set each ornament on a miniature grapevine wreath sprayed gold.

Rich red walls set the holiday stage in the dining room. Sparkling crystal and china, tall candles, and a centerpiece created just for the season complete the mood.

Lemon Leaf Wreath

These fragrant entryway flourishes will make your home smell like Christmas.

A scattering of **clove-studded fruit** and fresh greenery is spicy and traditional—and so much fun even the kids will want to help. Packages, decoratively displayed under the table, sport kraft paper wrappings, raffia ribbon, and **citrus and lemon leaf badges**. Wired ribbon makes perfect bows for the candles.

The pièce de résistance is a boldly dramatic dried **lemon leaf wreath**. To make the wreath, cut a diamond-shaped base from a ½"-thick sheet of Styrofoam. Using florist's pins, attach dried lemon leaf stalks to the base. Then hot-glue gilded lemon leaves randomly on the wreath. Attach a wire to the back of the base for hanging.

Clove-Studded Fruit

Citrus and Lemon Leaf Badges

Gilded Apples

The simplest gestures—fruit, flowers, greenery—are the very ones that impart the holiday spirit.

Gilded apples in a bowl boast the colors of the season—red, green, and gold. To gild, lightly spritz the apples with gold spray paint. When dry, nestle the gilded apples on sheet moss in a large decorative bowl. Tuck sprigs of fresh greenery in any gaps. If your bowl is especially large, start by placing crumpled newspaper in the bottom of the bowl; it takes up space and can easily be hidden by the apples and the greenery.

To make the **cinnamon candle**, hot-glue long cinnamon sticks around a large pillar candle. Tie a raffia bow around the candle and slip dried lemon leaves and citrus slices into the bow.

For this lush **greenery tieback**, we simply wrapped a length of purchased garland around the curtain and secured it at the back with florist's wire.

A delightful gift for any unexpected holiday visitor is a little cellophane-wrapped package of **paperwhite bulbs** that the recipient can coax into bloom. Tie bunches of the treats with festive ribbon and pile them in a pretty bowl to await your guests.

Cinnamon Candle

Greenery Tieback

Paperwhite Bulbs

13

Peppermint Tower

The **peppermint tower** that sits atop the coffee table in the keeping room may be just the project for older children to fill those long hours before Christmas arrives.

With adult supervision, insert a twig into the center of the bottom of a Styrofoam tree; then insert the opposite end of the twig into a block of Styrofoam that you have hot-glued in place in the bottom of a decorative pot. Hot-glue unwrapped peppermint candies to the Styrofoam tree form. Cover the top of the Styrofoam block with sheet moss and tie a fluffy bow around the tree's "trunk."

It isn't necessary for everything in your holiday setting to be red and green. Yards of plaid ribbon, dried citrus, cinnamon sticks, fresh greenery, Santa stockings, and nutcrackers go with anything. The painting above the mantel is in perfect harmony with the Christmas decorations.

Note: For many of the products featured here, see Sources on page 156.

The creative force behind all this Christmas magic is *Southern Living* Interiors Editor **Mary McWilliams**. When we arrived to photograph the house, it looked just like everyone's house does on decorating day—boxes, papers, and ornaments scattered everywhere! But in no time, Mary Mac and her merry crew had the house picture perfect for the holidays.

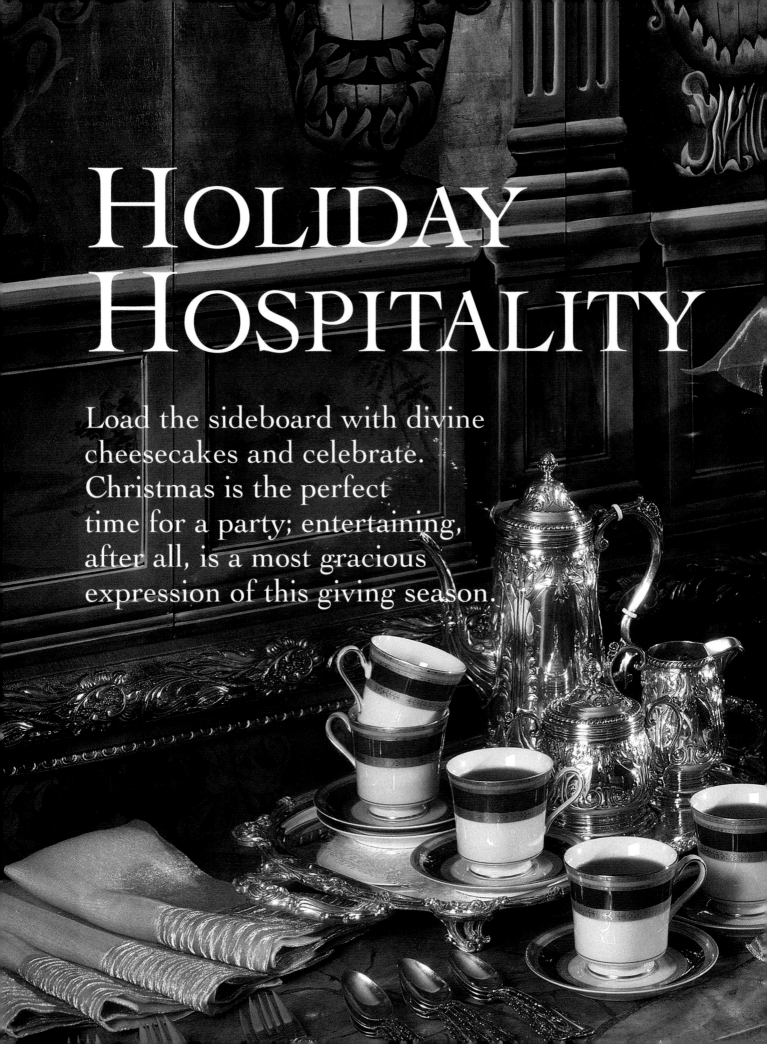

HOLIDAY HOSPITALITY

Load the sideboard with divine cheesecakes and celebrate. Christmas is the perfect time for a party; entertaining, after all, is a most gracious expression of this giving season.

Hot Fudge Cheesecake

Jeweled Cheesecake

Peppermint Stick Cheesecake

Tipsy Eggnog Cheesecake

An Elegant Cheesecake Party

Jeweled Cheesecake

Press the linens. Set out the silver and china. It's as easy as that to get ready for a party that looks and tastes like a celebration of the first order. To make matters even simpler, co-host the party with a friend.

Jeweled Cheesecake

For a delectable party favor, send a sliver of each cheesecake home with your guests.

2¼ cups gingersnap cookie
    crumbs
¼ cup plus 2 tablespoons
    butter or margarine,
    melted
⅔ cup whipping cream
1 pound white chocolate,
    finely chopped
4 (8-ounce) packages cream
    cheese, softened
1 cup sugar
6 large eggs
1 teaspoon vanilla extract
    Candied Cranberries
    (optional)
    Pistachio Crunch (optional)

Combine gingersnap crumbs and melted butter; stir well. Press crumb mixture into bottom and 1" up sides of a 10" springform pan. Bake at 350° for 10 minutes. Let cool. Reduce oven temperature to 300°.

Bring whipping cream to a simmer in a saucepan. Remove from heat and pour over chocolate in a large bowl. Stir mixture with a rubber spatula until smooth. Let cool.

Beat cream cheese at high speed of an electric mixer until creamy. Add sugar; beat well.

Add eggs, one at a time, beating after each addition. Fold in chocolate mixture. Stir in vanilla. Pour batter into prepared crust.

Bake at 300° for 1 hour and 15 minutes. Let cool completely on a wire rack. Cover and chill at least 8 hours. Remove sides of pan. If desired, decorate cheesecake with Candied Cranberries and Pistachio Crunch. **Yield:** one 10" cheesecake.

Candied Cranberries
2½ cups sugar
1 cup hot water
¾ cup cranberry-apple juice
    drink
3½ cups fresh cranberries

Combine first 3 ingredients in a small nonaluminum saucepan. Bring to a boil; reduce heat and simmer, uncovered, until sugar dissolves, stirring occasionally.

Remove from heat and pour syrup mixture over cranberries in a medium-size heatproof bowl. Place bowl on a steamer rack in a large Dutch oven over simmering water. Cover and steam 30 minutes. Remove bowl of cranberries. Let cool completely without stirring.

Cover bowl with cheesecloth; let stand at room temperature for 3 days, stirring occasionally. (Mixture will become thick.)

Transfer cranberries, using a slotted spoon, to a large mesh wire rack placed over a wax paper-lined jellyroll pan. Store cranberry syrup in a glass container in refrigerator for another use. Let fruit dry, uncovered, for 2 to 3 days, turning occasionally. Reserve ¼ cup Candied Cranberries for use in Pistachio Crunch. **Yield:** 2½ cups candied cranberries and 2 cups syrup.

Note: Candied Cranberries can be prepared and refrigerated up to 2 weeks ahead.

Pistachio Crunch
12 ounces vanilla-flavored
    candy coating
⅓ cup chopped, toasted
    pistachio nuts
¼ cup Candied Cranberries,
    chopped

Melt candy coating in a heavy saucepan over low heat, stirring constantly. Remove from heat.

Stir in nuts and cranberries. Spread mixture in a thick layer (about ¼") on a wax paper-lined baking sheet. Let cool completely. Break into pieces or use Christmas cookie cutters to cut desired shapes. **Yield:** 1 pound.

Hot Fudge Cheesecake

This dessert develops a brownie-like top as it bakes. Serve any leftover Hot Fudge Sauce over ice cream or pound cake.

    1 cup crushed saltine crackers
    ½ cup finely chopped walnuts
    ¼ cup plus 2 tablespoons
        butter or margarine, melted
    3 tablespoons sugar
    6 (1-ounce) squares semisweet
        chocolate
    ¾ cup butter or margarine
    1 (8-ounce) package cream
        cheese, softened
    ¾ cup sugar
    3 large eggs
        Hot Fudge Sauce
        Garnish: fresh mint sprigs

Combine first 4 ingredients; stir well. Firmly press onto bottom and 2½" up sides of a lightly greased 7" springform pan. Bake at 350° for 8 minutes. Remove to a wire rack; let cool. Reduce oven temperature to 300°.

Combine chocolate squares and ¾ cup butter in a heavy saucepan. Cook over medium-low heat until mixture is melted and smooth, stirring frequently. Remove from heat and let cool.

Beat cream cheese at medium speed of an electric mixer until creamy. Add ¾ cup sugar; beat well. Add eggs, one at a time, beating after each addition. Stir in cooled chocolate mixture. Pour into prepared crust.

Bake at 300° for 50 minutes to 1 hour or until almost set. Turn oven off. Let cheesecake cool in oven 30 minutes. Remove to a wire rack; let cool to room temperature.

Remove sides of pan. Serve cheesecake with Hot Fudge Sauce. Garnish, if desired. **Yield:** one 7" cheesecake.

Hot Fudge Sauce

    1 (12-ounce) package
        semisweet chocolate morsels
    1 cup half-and-half
    1 tablespoon butter or
        margarine
    1 teaspoon vanilla extract

Combine chocolate morsels and half-and-half in a heavy saucepan.

Cook over medium heat until chocolate melts and mixture is smooth, stirring frequently. Remove from heat; stir in butter and vanilla. Serve warm. **Yield:** 2 cups.

Sweet Potato-Coconut Streusel Cheesecake

Write the name of this regal cheesecake on shimmery ribbon.

    1¼ cups round buttery cracker
        crumbs
    ½ cup finely chopped pecans
    ⅓ cup flaked coconut
    ⅓ cup butter or margarine,
        melted
    ¼ cup all-purpose flour
    1 tablespoon brown sugar
    2 tablespoons butter or
        margarine
    ½ cup flaked coconut
    ½ cup pecan pieces
    3 (8-ounce) packages cream
        cheese, softened
    1 cup firmly packed brown
        sugar
    1 cup cooked, mashed sweet
        potato
    ½ cup Kahlúa or other
        coffee-flavored liqueur
    ¾ teaspoon ground cinnamon
    3 large eggs
        Garnishes: sweetened
        whipped cream, ground
        cinnamon

Combine first 4 ingredients; stir well. Firmly press crumb mixture onto bottom and 1" up sides of a 9" springform pan. Bake at 350° for 10 to 12 minutes. Remove to a wire rack; let cool. Reduce oven temperature to 325°.

Combine flour and 1 tablespoon brown sugar; then cut in

Hot Fudge Cheesecake

Sweet Potato-Coconut Streusel Cheesecake

2 tablespoons butter with a pastry blender until mixture is crumbly. Stir in ½ cup coconut and ½ cup pecan pieces. Set mixture aside.

Beat cream cheese at medium speed of an electric mixer until creamy; gradually add 1 cup brown sugar, beating well. Add sweet potato, Kahlúa, and ¾ teaspoon cinnamon; beat at low speed until blended. Add eggs, one at a time, beating after each addition. Pour batter into pre- pared crust.

Bake at 325° for 45 minutes. Remove cheesecake from oven and sprinkle coconut mixture over top. Bake 25 additional minutes. Let cheesecake cool to room tem- perature in pan on a wire rack.

Cover and chill. Before serving, remove sides of pan. Garnish, if desired. **Yield:** one 9" cheesecake.

Note: Sprinkling cinnamon over two intricately shaped forks offers an appetizing invitation to enjoy a luscious slice.

Peppermint Panache Cheesecake

Candy canes atop the cake hint at the crushed peppermints found in each slice.

2¼ cups cream-filled chocolate sandwich cookie crumbs
2 tablespoons butter or margarine, melted
4 (8-ounce) packages cream cheese, softened
1¼ cups sugar
½ cup whipping cream
2 tablespoons all-purpose flour
1 teaspoon vanilla extract
4 large eggs
1 cup coarsely chopped cream-filled chocolate sandwich cookies
⅓ cup coarsely crushed hard peppermint candies
10 ounces premium white chocolate, finely chopped
⅓ cup whipping cream
Garnish: small candy canes

Combine 2¼ cups cookie crumbs and butter; stir well. Firmly press onto bottom and 2" up sides of a 9" springform pan. Bake at 350° for 8 minutes. Remove to a wire rack; let cool. Reduce oven temperature to 325°.

Beat cream cheese at medium speed of an electric mixer until creamy; gradually add sugar, beating well. Add ½ cup whipping cream, flour, and vanilla; beat well. Add eggs, one at a time, beating after each addition. Stir in 1 cup chopped cookies and ⅓ cup crushed peppermint candies. Pour batter into prepared crust.

Bake at 325° for 1 hour or until almost set. Remove to a wire rack; let cool completely. Cover and chill at least 8 hours. Remove sides of springform pan.

Bring water to a boil in bottom of a double boiler; remove from heat. Combine white chocolate and ⅓ cup whipping cream in top of double boiler; place over hot water. Heat until chocolate is melted and smooth, stirring constantly with a rubber spatula. Let mixture cool slightly (3 to 5 minutes).

Spread white chocolate mixture over top and sides of cheesecake. Garnish with candy canes. **Yield:** one 9" cheesecake.

Tipsy Eggnog Cheesecake

You can store Sugared Rose Petals in an airtight container several months.

2 cups wheatmeal biscuit crumbs
⅓ cup butter or margarine, melted
2 tablespoons sugar
½ teaspoon ground nutmeg
3 (8-ounce) packages cream cheese, softened
1 cup sugar
1 tablespoon cornstarch
5 large eggs
¾ cup canned or homemade eggnog
¼ cup dark rum
¼ cup brandy
Sugared Rose Petals (optional)

Combine first 4 ingredients; stir well. Firmly press crumb mixture onto bottom and 1½" up sides of a lightly greased 9" springform pan. Bake at 325° for 12 to 15 minutes. Remove to a wire rack; let cool.

Beat cream cheese at medium speed of an electric mixer until creamy; gradually add 1 cup sugar and cornstarch, beating well. Add eggs, one at a time, beating after each addition. Stir in eggnog, rum, and brandy. Pour batter into prepared crust.

Bake at 325° for 1 hour. (Center will be soft.) Remove from oven and gently run a knife around edge of pan to release cheesecake from sides; return to oven. Turn oven off; leave cheesecake in oven, with oven door partially opened, 30 minutes. Let cool to room temperature in pan on a wire rack. Cover and chill 8 hours.

Remove sides of pan and top cheesecake with Sugared Rose Petals, if desired. **Yield:** one 9" cheesecake.

Sugared Rose Petals

3 large pesticide-free roses
¼ cup frozen egg substitute, thawed and lightly beaten
½ cup superfine sugar

Pull the petals free from one rose. Lightly coat each petal on both sides with egg substitute, using a small paintbrush.

Sift a small amount of sugar over the coated petals, turning them carefully to coat both sides. Set on wax paper to dry at least 1 hour. Repeat procedure with remaining roses, egg substitute, and sugar. **Yield:** 1½ cups.

Note: Substitute other edible flowers, if desired. Many grocery stores carry prepackaged edible flowers; see also Sources on page 156.

Tipsy Eggnog Cheesecake

Supper
After the
Shopping
Spree

The anticipation of
supper with friends
makes a day of
holiday shopping
more fun. Meet
over coffee to
finalize gift lists;
then gather late in
the afternoon to
wrap presents.

Christmas Spritzers

Christmas Spritzers

Turkey Pot Pies with Cornbread Crust

Spur-of-the-Moment Salad

Cranberry Parfaits

Tea   Coffee

Serve these refreshing berry spritzers as guests are busy tying bows on packages. Then pop the Turkey Pot Pies in the oven, toss the salad, and assemble the Cranberry Parfaits just before serving. The pot pie filling and parfait mixture can be prepared a day in advance.

Christmas Spritzers

   2 (12-ounce) cans frozen cranberry juice concentrate, thawed and undiluted
   2 (750-milliliter) bottles White Zinfandel, chilled
   ¼ cup Angostura bitters
   1 (10-ounce) bottle club soda, chilled
      Garnishes: maraschino cherries, orange curls

Combine first 3 ingredients in a pitcher. Cover and chill. Add club soda just before serving. Serve over ice. Garnish, if desired. **Yield:** 10½ cups.

Note: Substitute 2 (23-ounce) bottles chilled sparkling mineral water for wine, if desired.

Turkey Pot Pies with Cornbread Crust

Commercial cornbread dough makes a convenient, tasty pie topping.

> 3 large carrots, scraped and sliced
> 1 large baking potato, cubed
> 1 large onion, chopped
> ⅓ cup butter or margarine, melted
> ⅓ cup all-purpose flour
> 4 cups chicken broth or homemade turkey stock
> 4 cups coarsely chopped cooked turkey
> 1 (7-ounce) can mexicorn, undrained
> ¼ cup chopped cilantro or parsley
> 1 teaspoon coarsely ground pepper
> ¾ teaspoon salt
> 1 (15-ounce) can black beans, drained
> 1 (11.5-ounce) can refrigerated cornbread twists
> Garnish: fresh cilantro

Turkey Pot Pie with Cornbread Crust, Spur-of-the-Moment Salad

Cook carrot and potato in boiling water to cover 15 to 20 minutes or until tender. Drain and set aside.

Cook onion in butter in a Dutch oven over medium heat, stirring constantly, until tender. Gradually add flour, stirring until blended. Cook, stirring constantly, 1 minute. Gradually add broth; cook over medium heat, stirring constantly, until mixture is thickened and bubbly. Remove from heat.

Stir in vegetables, turkey, and next 4 ingredients. Cover and refrigerate overnight. (Mixture will become very thick.)

Reheat turkey mixture in Dutch oven over medium heat until thoroughly heated, stirring frequently. Stir in beans. Spoon turkey mixture evenly into 6 (2-cup) ovenproof soup bowls.

Unroll cornbread dough into 16 strips. Twist 2 strips together and place over each pot pie. (Bake remaining 4 strips for another use.)

Bake, uncovered, at 375° for 17 to 20 minutes or until cornbread is browned. Garnish, if desired. **Yield:** 6 servings.

Spur-of-the-Moment Salad

> 9 cups mixed salad greens
> ⅓ cup olive oil
> 2 tablespoons red wine vinegar
> ¾ teaspoon stone-ground mustard
> ¼ teaspoon sugar
> ¼ teaspoon salt
> ¼ teaspoon pepper
> 1½ cups commercial or homemade croutons
> Freshly ground pepper

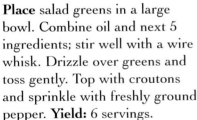

Cranberry Parfait

Place salad greens in a large bowl. Combine oil and next 5 ingredients; stir well with a wire whisk. Drizzle over greens and toss gently. Top with croutons and sprinkle with freshly ground pepper. **Yield:** 6 servings.

Note: Mixed salad greens come prepackaged in many grocery stores and farmer's markets. Or, you can clean and tear your own mix of greens in advance. Store with a damp paper towel in a large zip-top plastic bag in the refrigerator.

Cranberry Parfaits

2 cups fresh or frozen
    cranberries, thawed
2 cups miniature
    marshmallows
¾ cup sugar
2 cups chopped apple
1 cup frozen whipped
    topping, thawed
2 (3-ounce) packages cream
    cheese, softened
⅓ cup cream of coconut
2 tablespoons powdered sugar
¾ cup granola cereal without
    raisins

Position knife blade in food processor bowl; add cranberries. Pulse until cranberries are chopped. Combine cranberries, marshmallows, and ¾ cup sugar in a bowl, stirring gently. Cover and chill at least 2 hours.

Fold in apple and whipped topping. Spoon mixture into 6 (4-ounce) parfait glasses, filling ¾ full. Beat cream cheese, cream of coconut, and powdered sugar at medium speed of an electric mixer until smooth. Top parfaits with cream cheese mixture. Sprinkle with granola. **Yield:** 6 servings.

THE FESTIVE TABLE

'Tis the season for peppermints, candy canes, and whimsy of the sweetest sort. When you make a Christmas confection of the table setting, you'll soon be serving up smiles.

Playful Partyware

Create some fun with candy cane shades of yellow, green, and red.

Apple Tree

Colorful apples, peppermint candies, and gingham ribbon work together to create a whimsical look that will make your festive setting sparkle. For the ribbon and the beeswax candles, see Sources on page 156.

Apple Tree

Push wooden florist's picks into the bottom of red, green, and yellow apples; then insert them into a 10"-tall Styrofoam cone. Tuck in sprigs of greenery and holly. Wire loops of ribbon to florist's picks and insert the ribbon among the apples.

Peppermint Pots

Hot-glue peppermint candies around the rim of tiny terra-cotta pots. Drop melted wax into the bottom of each pot and insert a bright beeswax candle. Tuck in sprigs of greenery around the base of each candle.

Peppermint-Stick Vase

Hot-glue peppermint candy sticks around a coffee can for a quick vase with charming appeal.

Candy Candles

For unique votive candle holders, hot-glue peppermint candies to the outside of assorted water and wine glasses. Accent with gingham ribbons. (To reuse the glasses, simply pry off the candy with your fingers.)

Peppermint Pots

Peppermint-Stick Vase

Candy Candles

Floral Tabletop Garland

Gather fresh greenery from your yard to begin a lush centerpiece you can make in an hour. Floral designer Peggy Barnhart shows you how.

You will need:
large sheet of plastic (to protect work surface)
1 yard 1'-wide chicken wire
1 yard florist's foil
3 florist's foam bricks, each cut in half and soaked in water
green sheet moss
florist's wire and picks
clippers
desired greenery (variegated ivy, holly, and Chinese evergreen shown)
desired fresh-cut flowers and fruits (red tulips, white lilies, red peppers, and green apples shown)
2 yards 2"-wide sheer gold wired ribbon

Note: Garland pictured is approximately 10" x 30".

1. On plastic sheet, stack chicken wire and florist's foil. Alternately place 5 foam pieces and moss along center of foil (reserve remaining foam piece for another use). Cut foil 1½" larger on all sides than foam.

2. Fold up foil twice around sides of foam to form a tray to hold water. Fold up chicken wire around foam and secure with florist's wire. If desired, form foam base into serpentine shape.

3. Cut stems of greenery 5" to 7" long. Insert stems into base, covering base completely. Leave some pieces longer and allow them to trail out from ends of arrangement.

4. Cut flower stems 8" to 10" long. Insert stems into base. Use picks to pierce bottoms of apples and to attach peppers; insert into base. Cut ribbon into 3 (24") lengths. Form each length into a loop with tails and attach loops to base with picks.

Peggy Barnhart of Birmingham, Alabama, frequently makes this centerpiece for special occasions: "I love this arrangement because it's low enough for guests to talk across the table."

33

Holiday Showpieces

Give ordinary glassware a glamorous make-over
simply by gluing on colorful glass gems.

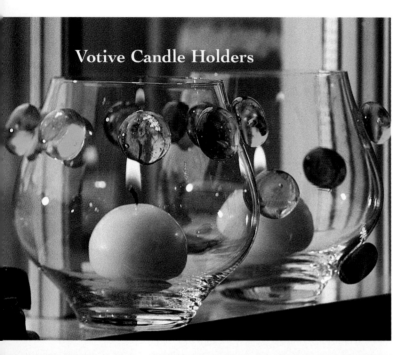

Votive Candle Holders

You will need:
assorted clear glassware
clear silicone (Creatively yours™ or Duro™
  from Loctite)
ruby red and emerald green glass gems

  Note: For glass gems, votive holders, candles, and
silicone, see Sources on page 156.
  1. Thoroughly clean and dry glassware.
  2. For each piece, referring to manufacturer's
directions, put drop of silicone on flat side of 1 glass
gem; press gem firmly against glass in desired position. Hold in place for a few seconds to let glue set.
Repeat for remaining gems. (Place gems on areas of
glassware that will not come in direct contact with
food.)
  3. Let pieces dry for 24 hours. Hand-wash
glassware to clean.

Wineglasses

Bowl and Platter

Boxwood Tree

Holly Tree

Juniper Tree

Fraser Fir Tree

Holly Tree

NATURE'S GREETINGS

It's one of the season's most enduring symbols, the hardy evergreen. Even the smallest measure—like these verdant topiaries—brings a bit of the holiday spirit into your home.

To make an enchanting **topiary**, pretreat greenery clippings by soaking them overnight in tepid water; then spray-paint a 12"- or 14"-tall Styrofoam cone dark green and let dry. Using florist's pins, attach greenery to the cone, concealing the pins. If desired, hot-glue tiny ornaments or berries to your tree. To keep the tree fresh, mist every few days.

We like the look created by making several trees from different types of greenery and grouping them on a table or a deep window ledge. To give our miniature forest a little more stature, we varied the heights by placing some trees on stacked, painted terra-cotta saucers. For the tree in the foreground, a column capital makes a fitting pedestal.

A Gardener's Wreath

Present bulbs on a purchased wreath for a gift that will be admired long after the season. After planting the bulbs, the recipient can enjoy the fragrant blooms.

You will need:
7 yards ⅛"-wide silver-and-gold ribbon
24 paperwhite bulbs
short straight pins (optional)
florist's wire
4 lily bulbs
grapevine or other rambling vine
1 (18"-diameter) fresh evergreen wreath
2 yards 2"-wide gold sheer ribbon (optional)

Note: For bulbs and evergreen wreath, see Sources on page 156.

1. Cut silver-and-gold ribbon into 18 (14") lengths. Wrap 18 paperwhite bulbs each with a length of ribbon, using short straight pins, if necessary, to secure ribbon to bulbs.

2. Cut 18 (8") lengths of florist's wire. Run wire through back of ribbon-wrapped bulbs and wire to wreath as desired. Wrap remaining paperwhite bulbs and lily bulbs in wire and attach securely to wreath.

3. Wire long lengths of grapevine (we took ours from a grapevine wreath) randomly around wreath. If desired, make a 4-loop bow from gold ribbon and wire to wreath.

4. Place wreath outdoors to ensure bulbs will remain healthy for later planting.

Hydrangeas for the Holidays

This lovely garland and wreath take advantage of the fluffy, snowy blooms of hydrangeas clipped at their peak in mid to late summer. Plan ahead for Christmas by drying the blooms and saving them for winter decorations.

You will need:
dried hydrangea stems
dried eucalyptus stalks with flowers
dried lemon leaf stalks
florist's wire
purchased fresh greenery garland or wreath

1. Cut dried hydrangea, eucalyptus, and lemon leaf stems to approximately 5" long.
2. Using florist's wire, tuck a few eucalyptus and lemon leaf stalks around a hydrangea bloom to form individual clusters.
3. Using florist's wire, attach clusters securely to garland or wreath.
4. Garland and wreath will not hold up in inclement weather. They are best used as indoor decorations or in covered outdoor areas.

Drying Hydrangeas

• Mophead, peegee, and oakleaf hydrangeas are particularly well suited for drying. Mophead varieties yield deep blue, purple, and pink blooms that dry to mellowed hues of these colors; peegee and oakleaf blooms dry to brown and burgundy.
• Cut the blooms from the bush after they have begun to dry naturally; the petals should have begun to stiffen slightly. (Picking too soon results in wilted blooms.)
• Always pick more than you think you'll need; some blooms will not dry as successfully as others.

• Strip all of the leaves from the stems.
• Bundle the hydrangea stems in groups of three or four and hang them upside down in a warm, dry, dark place for several weeks to dry.
• Once dry, lightly spray the blooms with an inexpensive aerosol hair spray to prevent the blooms from deteriorating.
• If you don't have a hydrangea bush, plant one (they're easy to maintain) or ask a neighbor for clippings. Or for dried hydrangea blooms, see Sources on page 156.

Make Your Tree a Star

Whether you use black-eyed peas or bright berries, this tree topper is one of a kind.

You will need (for 1 star):
Styrofoam star
18" florist's pick
silver metallic spray paint (Design Master™ used)
hot-glue gun with glue sticks
desired covering: dried black-eyed peas, Chinese tallow berries, or Florida berries
silver metallic wax finish (Treasure Gold® used)
small paintbrush
florist's wire

Note: For Styrofoam star and berries, see Sources on page 156.

1. Insert florist's pick into bottom of star. Spray entire star silver. Let dry.

2. Referring to photo and working from center to outer points of star, hot-glue peas or berries to ridges of star. On slopes between ridges, working from center to outer points of star, hot-glue peas or berries in rows covering surface of star. Let dry. Turn star over and repeat for opposite side.

3. For black-eyed pea star, referring to photo, brush silver wax craft paint onto star, covering completely. Let dry.

4. To attach star to tree top, position florist's pick against tree trunk. Wrap florist's wire around pick and trunk until star is secure.

Floral artist **Lyman Ratcliffe** of Houston, Texas, uses materials with special holiday meaning to adorn his tree toppers. "In the South, black-eyed peas are thought to bring luck in the new year, so why not top your tree with them?"

43

DECORATIONS TO MAKE

Plain or fancy, the best
Christmas ornaments
are the ones you've
crafted yourself. This
tree skirt and its
matching ornaments
convey that handmade,
heartfelt sentiment.

Starry Night
Cut-Ups for the Tree

Rival the heavens with this brilliant no-sew tree skirt
and matching ornaments in out-of-this world colors.

Tree Skirt

You will need:
patterns and diagram on page 148
tracing paper
9" x 12" felt sheets: 4 gold, 4 kelly green, 4 apple
   green, 8 hunter green, 4 chartreuse
54"-diameter precut red felt circle or 1½ yards
   54"-wide red felt
pushpin
1 yard string
dressmaker's chalk
thick craft glue
1⅓ yards 1"-wide gold ribbon

Note: Finished skirt is 54" in diameter. For precut
felt circle and felt sheets, see Sources on page 156.

1. Using tracing paper, transfer patterns to felt
and cut out as indicated.

2. If using precut circle, find center of skirt by
folding circle into fourths. Mark and cut out a 6"-
diameter circle at center. Cut straight line from outer
edge to inner circle for opening.

If using uncut felt, referring to Cutting Diagram
on page 148, fold felt in half and then in half again.
To mark outer circle, tie pushpin to end of string.
Stick pushpin through corner of felt where folds
meet. Measure and mark 27" from
pushpin. Tie loose end of string to
dressmaker's chalk at this mark.
Holding string taut, draw arc with
27" radius. To mark inner circle,
draw arc with 3" radius in same
manner. Cut along marked lines
through all layers; open skirt. Cut
straight line from outer edge to
inner circle for skirt opening.

3. Referring to photo, glue
trees to top of skirt. Then glue
stars and moon to top of skirt.

4. For ties, cut 4 (12") pieces
of ribbon. Referring to photo on
page 44, on wrong side of skirt,
glue 1 end each of 2 ribbons to
each side of opening. Let dry. Tie
ribbons together to close skirt.

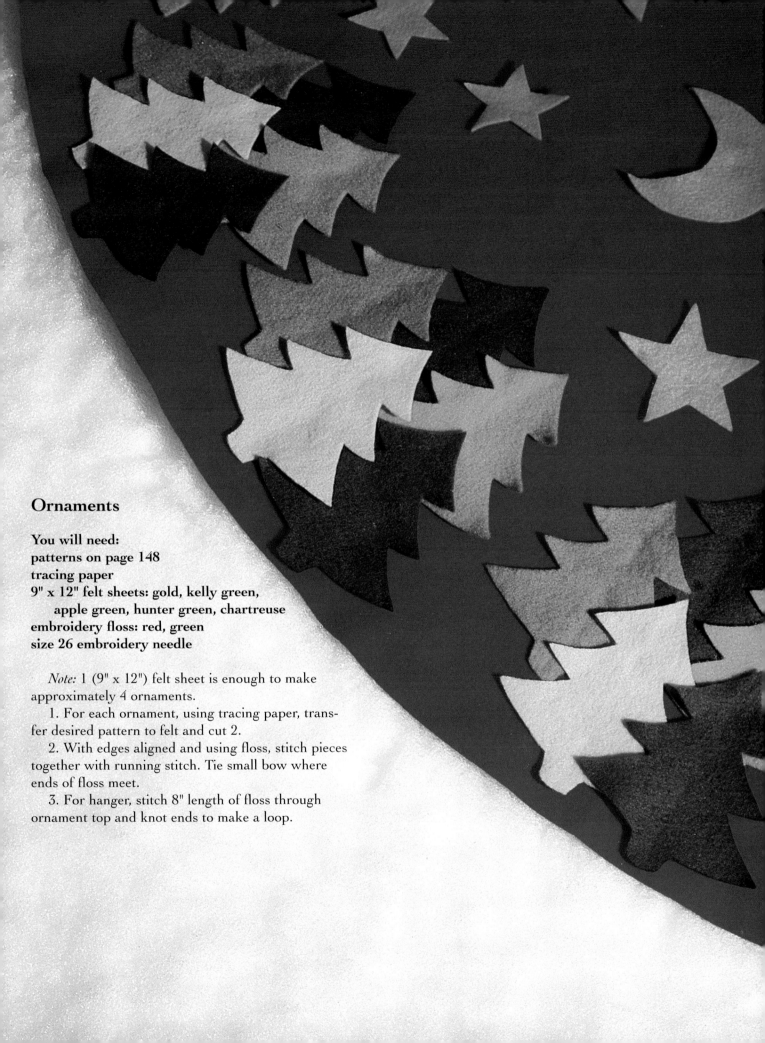

Ornaments

You will need:
patterns on page 148
tracing paper
9" x 12" felt sheets: gold, kelly green,
**   apple green, hunter green, chartreuse**
embroidery floss: red, green
size 26 embroidery needle

Note: 1 (9" x 12") felt sheet is enough to make approximately 4 ornaments.

1. For each ornament, using tracing paper, transfer desired pattern to felt and cut 2.

2. With edges aligned and using floss, stitch pieces together with running stitch. Tie small bow where ends of floss meet.

3. For hanger, stitch 8" length of floss through ornament top and knot ends to make a loop.

Toile-la-la Stockings

Mix and match traditional toile fabrics with lively checks.

You will need (for 1 stocking):
patterns on page 149
tracing paper
½ yard fabric for stocking
1 yard contrasting fabric for lining, flap, and
    piping
1⅓ yards ¼" cording for corded piping
thread to match fabrics and trim
desired trim: 12" length ⅛" upholstery cording to
    match fabrics and 3" tassel to match cording
    or 1 (1¼") mother-of-pearl button

Note: Patterns include ½" seam allowances. For fabrics, see Sources on page 156.

1. Using tracing paper, enlarge and transfer stocking pattern to stocking fabric. Cut 1; reverse and cut 1 more. Repeat to cut lining fabric. Transfer flap pattern to flap fabric and cut 4. (Stocking has front and back flap.)

2. For corded piping, from remaining lining fabric, cut 2½"-wide strips. With right sides facing and raw edges aligned, stitch strips together to make 1⅓ yards; press. Lay cording in center of wrong side of strip. With wrong sides facing and raw edges aligned, fold strip in half to encase cording. Stitch along cording edge. Trim raw edges to ½".

3. With right sides facing and raw edges aligned, stitch 2 flap pieces together along bottom edges, leaving sides and top open. Clip corner, turn, and press. Repeat for remaining flap.

4. Position 1 flap on right side of stocking front, aligning top and side edges. Repeat with remaining flap and stocking back. With raw edges aligned, pin corded piping to right side of stocking front around sides and bottom. With right sides facing and

raw edges aligned, stitch stocking pieces together, catching piping and flaps in seam and leaving top open. Clip curves and turn.

5. For hanger, cut 1 (2" x 4") strip from lining fabric. With right sides facing and raw edges aligned, fold strip in half lengthwise. Stitch long raw edges together; turn. Fold hanger in half to make a loop. With raw edges aligned, baste hanger to right side of stocking back at top corner above heel.

6. For lining, with right sides facing and raw edges aligned, stitch lining pieces together, leaving top edge open and large opening in side seam above heel. Clip curves but do not turn.

7. With right sides facing, slide lining over stocking, matching side seams. With raw edges aligned and loop toward center, stitch around top edge of stocking, securing hanger in seam. Turn through opening in lining. Slipstitch opening closed. Tuck lining inside stocking.

8. Add finishing accent to flap: For medallion, wind cording into coil, stitching to secure. With tassel underneath, center medallion ½" above point of flap and stitch in place. Or center button ½" above point of flap and stitch in place.

Celestial Centerpiece

This simple woodworking project—a snap to cut out and paint—has its heart in folk art.

This angel is sure to become a family favorite. Even the children can help paint it. Made from two separate wooden pieces, the angel comes apart and lies flat for easy storage.

You will need:
patterns on pages 150-151
tracing paper
4" square white posterboard
32" length 1 x 10 pine board
band saw or jigsaw
sandpaper
liquid gesso
carbon paper
small and medium paintbrushes
acrylic enamel paint (DecoArt™ UltraGloss used): red, white
acrylic paint (DecoArt™ Americana used): medium peach, gold
fine-tip permanent brown marker
7" (18-gauge) brass wire
craft glue
gold dimensional paint (Tulip Colorpoint™ used)
drill with ¹⁄₁₆" bit

Note: For paints, see Sources on page 156.

1. Using tracing paper, transfer star and halo patterns to posterboard as indicated and cut out. Transfer outline of angel patterns to wood and cut out. From remaining wood, cut 1 (6½") square and 1 (5½") square for base. Sand all wood edges smooth. Apply 2 coats of gesso to all wood pieces, letting dry and then sanding after each coat.

2. Using carbon paper, transfer pattern markings to angel pieces. Referring to patterns and using 2 coats of enamel paint, paint the following: Paint dress and 6½" square red. Paint wings and 5½" square white. Let paint coats dry between applications.

Referring to pattern and using 2 coats of acrylic paint, paint the following: Paint face and hands peach. Paint collar, bands at wrist, bottom of dress, and head sides and back gold. Let paint coats dry between applications.

Paint stars on bands at bottom of dress with 1 coat of gesso and then 1 coat of white enamel, letting dry between applications.

3. Using carbon paper, transfer facial features to face. Using brown marker, trace features.

4. For large star, cut 3" length from brass wire. Referring to pattern, sandwich wire between 2 stars and glue. For halo, cut 2 (2") lengths from remaining brass wire. Referring to pattern, sandwich wire between 2 halo pieces and glue. Let dry. Paint halo gold.

5. Referring to photo, embellish angel with dimensional paint: add highlights on wings; add dots to corners of all stars and randomly to halo. Let dry.

6. Referring to pattern, drill 2 holes in top of angel's head and 1 in top of hand. Insert halo and star into holes as indicated. Slide angel front and side together and stack on top of bases as shown in photo.

Marvelous Mantels

Since the fireplace is a focal point this time of year, dress the mantel in something dashing for the holidays.

Striped Swag

e've created three distinctive looks to suit any taste—a sophisticated striped swag, shown at left, as well as a Victorian rose garland and a wintery snowflake valance shown on the following pages.

Striped Swag

You will need:
diagrams on page 152
1¼ yards 45"-wide medium-weight striped fabric for top
1¼ yards 45"-wide coordinating medium-weight fabric for backing
1¼ yards 45"-wide felt interlining
thread to match fabrics
dressmaker's pencil
6 small plastic rings
6 small cup hooks

Note: This pattern fits mantel 60" to 70" long. All seam allowances are ½". For striped fabric, see Sources on page 156.

1. From striped fabric, referring to Diagram 1, cut 2 (20½" x 45") lengths. With right sides facing and raw edges aligned, stitch lengths together along 1 short edge, positioning stripes so that pattern is continuous. Trim length of joined fabrics to 86", centering seam. Repeat for backing and interlining fabrics, offsetting seams to reduce bulk at center.

2. Referring to Diagram 2 and using dressmaker's pencil and ruler, on wrong side of striped fabric, draw horizontal line 6½" from bottom raw edge. Measure and mark points at indicated intervals along horizontal line. Along bottom edge, mark center of each 17" interval as indicated. (*Note:* Fabric stripes should be centered within points. If these measurements do not work well with your chosen striped fabric, make adjustments as needed.) Draw zigzagging lines connecting points and cut out. Use this as pattern to cut backing and interlining.

(Continued on page 54)

Rose Garland

3. Aligning raw edges, stack interlining, backing (right side up), and striped top (right side down). Pin. Stitch layers together, leaving large opening along straight edge for turning. Trim seams and clip corners. Turn and press. Blindstitch opening closed.

4. On wrong side of mantel swag, ½" from top edge, stitch plastic rings at left and right edges and at 17" intervals in between (plastic rings should be aligned in between points).

5. To hang swag, divide length of mantel by 5 (number of points on swag). Screw cup hooks underneath mantel shelf at intervals of this measurement, beginning at left end. For example, for 65"-long mantel, cup hooks would be placed 13" apart. Slip plastic rings over cup hooks.

Snowflake Valance

Bring roses and snowflakes to your holiday home with these charming embellishments for your mantel.

Snowflake Valance and Ornaments

You will need:
pattern on page 149
tracing paper
heavyweight paper
36"-wide white polyester felt (See Step 2 below to determine yardage.)
water-soluble pen
small, sharp scissors
1 packet 3-mm off-white round pearl beads
1 packet 4-mm off-white round pearl beads
1 packet 6-mm off-white oval pearl beads
thick craft glue

1. Using tracing paper, transfer snowflake pattern and markings to heavyweight paper and cut out.

2. Measure length of mantel shelf and cut white felt to this measurement. Measure depth of shelf and add 10"; trim width of felt to this measurement.

3. Starting at center of felt, place point A of pattern on bottom edge; points B and D should be equidistant from bottom edge. Using water-soluble pen, transfer snowflake pattern and markings. Repeat, working outward from center and adjusting placement of snowflakes as needed to allow for whole snowflake at each end.

4. Cut out bottom contour of snowflakes, removing water-soluble pen marks. To cut out interior shapes of each snowflake, referring to pattern markings, fold snowflake along dashed line B/D; cut out shapes along that fold, using small scissors. Refold snowflake along remaining dashed lines, 1 at a time, cutting out all interior shapes. Following manufacturer's directions, remove any remaining pen markings. Let dry and press.

5. Referring to pattern and using craft glue, glue beads to snowflakes. Referring to photo and beginning 10" up from bottom edge of valance, randomly glue additional beads above snowflakes. Let dry.

6. To make matching ornaments from remaining felt (see photo on page 149), cut 5" square from felt for each and fold square in half. Using lower half of snowflake pattern (with contoured outline), fold pattern in half along B/D line and align with folded edge of felt. Using water-soluble pen, transfer pattern and markings to felt and cut out. Glue on beads as for valance.

Rose Garland

You will need (for 6 roses):
diagrams on page 153
½ yard 45"-wide fabric or 4 yards 2"-wide ribbon
thread to match fabric
6 (10") lengths craft wire
½"-wide green floral craft tape

Note: To make 30 flowers as in photo, you will need ½ yard each of 4 different fabrics and 4 yards of 2"-wide organdy ribbon. (We used shades of maroon in velvet, pleated polyester, and organdy; rose sand-washed silk; and pink organdy ribbon.)

1. For fabric roses, cut 6 (4" x 23") bias strips from fabric. (If desired, cut 2 (4" x 19") bias strips from remaining fabric to make smaller roses.) Fold each strip in half lengthwise and trim ends diagonally (Diagram 1).

2. For each rose, working ¼" from edge, run gathering stitches down right edge and along bottom edge of folded strip (Diagram 2). Pull thread to gather tightly (Diagram 3). Roll gathered fabric into rosette, tacking every 3" to 4" at seam allowance to secure.

3. To add stem, wrap wire tightly around gathered base of rose. Twist end around wire "stem" to secure. Beginning at top of stem and working toward bottom, wrap wire with floral tape.

Note: For thick fabrics such as velvet, make small hook at 1 end of wire. Insert opposite end through rose from top to bottom; pull wire down until hook lodges above rose base (Diagram 4). Wrap stem with tape as above.

4. Tuck roses into fresh greenery garland.

Tassel Dazzle
These gorgeous trimmings are a visual delight.

These dramatic tassels are coveted both for their unusual fabrics and trims and their generous size. (The tassels at right are approximately 14" long.) They were made by Judy Ford, a self-taught artist and textile designer in Jackson, Mississippi, who has a national following. Judy hand-prints breathtaking velvet and silk fabrics in her warehouse-district studio. It's these fabrics that she uses to create her glamorous, opulent tassels.

To make Judy's signature tassels, follow her step-by-step instructions on pages 58 and 59. Substitute lengths of raffia and jute string or colorful upholstery cording for the metallic silk fabric as desired.

Raffia and Jute Tassel

Upholstery Cording Tassel

Crushed Metallic Silk Tassel

In her showroom in Jackson, Mississippi, Judy Ford is surrounded by the fruits of her labor.

J udy and her clients love the tassels for their many decorating and gift possibilites. "I put them all over my house," Judy says. "They add a personality of their own to the simplest piece of furniture." A few of her ideas:

— Hang a tassel from the neck of a lamp so that the top of the tassel is slightly below the bottom of the lampshade. Or loop it around the top of the lamp and let it drape over the front of the shade.

— For creative napkin rings, tie the tails of tassels around napkins and place a napkin in the center of each plate at your next formal party.

— Attach a tassel to a simple curtain tieback.

— Dangle a tassel from a chandelier.

— Accent a chifforobe or chest of drawers with a tassel hanging from the top drawer pull.

— Top a special present with a tassel or simply wrap the tassel as a gift itself.

Making a Tassel

You will need (for 14"-long tassel):
1⅝ yards (approximately 16"-wide) crushed
    metallic silk or polyester
1 yard gold metallic upholstery cording
liquid ravel preventer
4 yards Kreinik #002 metallic gold braid
flat head screwdriver or knitting needle
desired embellishment

1. Trim selvages from silk fabric and cut 2 (28") lengths. With right sides up and raw edges aligned, stack lengths.

2. Gather fabric pieces at center and twist pieces together. Center upholstery cording on twisted fabrics and tie a tight knot around fabrics. Apply liquid ravel preventer to each end of cording and knot each end. Continue to twist fabric very tightly, overlapping as shown.

3. To form neck of tassel, tie gold braid in a tight knot 2½" from top of tassel. Leave 5" tail in braid. Wrap braid upward very tightly around tassel for 1", covering fabric completely; then wrap back down to starting point.

4. Tie braid tails in a double knot. Cut tails to ¾".

5. Using screwdriver or knitting needle, tuck braid tails underneath tassel neck.

6. Cut fabric into ¼"-wide strips, stopping within ¼" of tassel neck. (*Note:* This will not be necessary if you are using individual threads or fibers as in other 2 tassels on page 57.) Stitch or glue desired embellishment to front of tassel at neck. Judy chose a chandelier prism found at a local flea market for this tassel.

For a quick gift or a package topper, this tassel takes the prize: Judy simply brushed a purchased tassel with gold fabric paint. She then added the heart charm to give it a bit of dash.

A Merry Welcome

Stencil these prancing reindeer on a coir doormat for a happy holiday greeting.

You will need:
pattern on page 152
8½" x 11" sheet clear, adhesive-backed plastic template material (available at art and office supply stores)
craft knife and protective mat or cardboard
natural coir outdoor mat
2"-wide clear packing tape
spray paints: red, white, green
acrylic paints: red, white
small round paintbrush
small stencil brush

Note: Mat shown is approximately 18" x 29".

1. Trace reindeer pattern onto sheet of plastic. Place sheet on protective mat and cut out stencil using craft knife.

2. For red border, use packing tape and several sheets of newspaper to cover center of mat, leaving 3" border at top and bottom and 2½" border at sides uncovered. Spray outer border red, pointing can directly down at mat to prevent paint from creeping under cover. Remove cover and let dry.

3. For white border, use packing tape and several sheets of newspaper to cover red border and center of mat, leaving ½" border next to red border. Spray inner border white. Remove cover and let dry.

4. Peel backing off plastic stencil. Referring to photo, position reindeer stencil in center of mat. Cover entire mat except stencil. Spray reindeer green. Remove cover and let dry. Repeat for remaining 2 reindeer. Using round paintbrush, paint noses and eyes red. Using stencil brush and white paint, add snowflakes. Let dry.

Stencil Magic

One simple pattern gives
you loads of terrific projects.
You'll marvel at how
they all add up.

Table Scarf

Gift Wraps

Turn plain papers and tissues into showstopping gift wraps.

Using the simple patterns on page 153 and gold paint, stencil desired holly-and-berry patterns onto assorted kraft papers, bags, and tissues. Refer to Stenciling Instructions on page 64.

For the holly gift tag, glue 2 pieces of kraft paper together and stencil a large holly leaf on the front. Let dry; then cut out around the leaf. Punch a hole in the tag and tie on with gold cord.

Pillow

You will need (for all projects):
stencil patterns on page 153
2 (8½" x 11") sheets plastic template material
craft knife and protective mat or cardboard
waxed paper (to protect work surface)
gold acrylic fabric paint (DecoArt™ Dazzling
    Metallics Glorious Gold used)
small and large stencil brushes
thread to match fabrics
4 (3") gold tassels (for pillow)
14" square pillow form (for pillow)

Stenciling Instructions

1. Trace desired stencil patterns onto frosted side of 1 sheet of plastic. Reverse holly pattern and trace onto remaining sheet of plastic. Place plastic, shiny side up, on protective mat and cut out stencils using craft knife.

2. Tape large pieces of waxed paper to work surface. If desired, practice stenciling on muslin scraps before beginning project. Periodically wash and dry stencils to prevent smudges. Move material to clean area of waxed paper before beginning new stencil.

3. Place material to be stenciled on top of waxed paper. Using stencil brushes and paint, stencil patterns onto material. Most projects shown are stenciled with groupings of 2 holly leaves (second leaf is reversed pattern) and 3 berries. Let dry.

Table Scarf

Note: We used 1½ yards 54"-wide white silk organza for a finished 47¾" square.

1. Turn raw edges of white silk organza under ⅛" and stitch; then turn edges under 3" and stitch hem, mitering corners. Press.

2. Referring to photo and working 4" from edge, stencil 3 large holly-and-berry groupings along 1 side of square. Continue pattern along remaining sides. Let dry.

Pillow

Note: We used ½ yard 45"-wide red crushed velvet for a finished 14" square. Seam allowance is ¼".

1. From red crushed velvet, cut 2 (14½"-square) pieces (or size to fit desired size pillow form).

2. Stencil 1 large holly-and-berry grouping in center of 1 velvet square. Let dry.

3. With right sides facing and raw edges aligned, stitch pillow front and back together, leaving large opening. Clip corners and turn. Insert pillow form. Slipstitch opening closed. Tack 1 purchased gold tassel to each corner of pillow.

Place Mats and Napkins

Note: We used 4 purchased cotton place mats. For 4 napkins, we used 1¼ yards 45"-wide white cotton organdy.

1. For each place mat, referring to photo, stencil small holly-and-berry patterns in each corner. Let dry.

2. For each napkin, from white cotton organdy, cut 1 (22") square. Turn raw edges under ⅛" and stitch; then turn edges under 1½" and stitch hem, mitering corners.

3. Stencil large holly-and-berry patterns in center of each napkin. Let dry.

Hand Towels

Referring to photo, stencil small holly-and-berry patterns onto purchased linen or cotton hand towels, as desired. Let dry.

Place Mat and Napkin

Hand Towels

A Jolly Santa to Stitch

Bearing a basket of Christmas joys, this cross-stitched Santa will warm your heart and hearth.

The framed cross-stitch piece is heirloom-worthy, a treasure to bring out Christmas after Christmas. If you're in the mood for a smaller project, the tiny, quick-to-stitch ornaments make wonderful package toppers.

Santa

You will need:
chart and color key on pages 154-155
17" square 14-count off-white Aida cloth
size 24 tapestry needle
embroidery floss (see color key)

Note: Finished design size is 10¾" square. For floss and fabric, see Sources on page 156.

1. Using 2 strands of floss and stitching over 1 thread, center and work cross-stitch design on Aida according to chart. For snow, use 2 strands each of floss and blending filament. For stars and borders, use whole gold braid. For backstitching, use 1 strand of floss.

2. With design centered, frame finished piece as desired.

Ornaments

You will need (for 12 ornaments):
charts and color key on page 154-155
8½" x 11" sheet 14-count red perforated paper
size 24 tapestry needle
embroidery floss (see color key)

Note: Finished design size for each is 1½" square. For floss and paper, see Sources on page 156.

1. For each ornament, cut 2½" square from paper. Using 2 strands of floss and stitching over 1 mesh, center and work desired cross-stitch design on paper square according to chart.

2. Cut out ornament 1 hole outside design, being careful not to cut into any hole holding a stitch.

3. To make hanger, thread 8" length of floss through center top of ornament and knot ends.

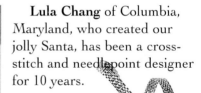

Lula Chang of Columbia, Maryland, who created our jolly Santa, has been a cross-stitch and needlepoint designer for 10 years.

Floral Fancies

Dried flowers and moss make these dainty ornaments natural keepsakes.

You will need:
3" to 4" Styrofoam shapes: heart, wreath, bell, star, ball
assorted ribbons
U-shaped florist's pins
hot-glue gun with glue sticks
green moss
gold crinkle wire
dried flowers (rosebuds, rose petals, freeze-dried pansies, globe amaranth, pepperberries, chrysanthemum petals, and daisies shown)
thick craft glue

Note: For Styrofoam shapes, crinkle wire, dried and freeze-dried flowers, see Sources on page 156.

For All Ornaments

1. For hanger, cut 8" to 10" length of ribbon; knot ends to make loop. Attach center of loop to center top of Styrofoam shape, using florist's pin.
2. Using hot glue, cover shape entirely with moss, concealing pin.
3. If desired, pin bow to top of ornament.

Wreath Ornament

Hot-glue pepperberry bunches to front of wreath. Referring to photo, hot-glue rosebuds and petals to wreath.

Note: To dry your own rose petals, place 3 paper towels on microwave-safe plate; arrange fresh rose petals in single layer on top and cover with paper towel. Microwave on HIGH for 3 minutes. Check petals for dryness; replace paper towels when moist. Continue microwaving at 30-second intervals, checking for desired dryness.

Wreath Ornament

Heart Ornament

1. Wrap crinkle wire around heart, securing ends with drop of craft glue.

2. Referring to photo and working from edge of heart inward, hot-glue rose petals to front of heart. Hot-glue pansy to center of rose petals.

Star Ornament

1. Wrap crinkle wire around star, securing ends with craft glue.

2. Referring to photo and working from outer edge inward, hot-glue rose petals to front of star. Hot-glue daisy to center of rose petals.

Ball Ornament

1. Wrap crinkle wire around ball, securing ends with craft glue.

2. Referring to photo and using craft glue, attach chrysanthemum petals in star formations to ball. Glue 1 rosebud to center of each star.

Bell Ornament

Referring to photo, hot-glue rose petals to bell. Hot-glue globe amaranth among rose petals.

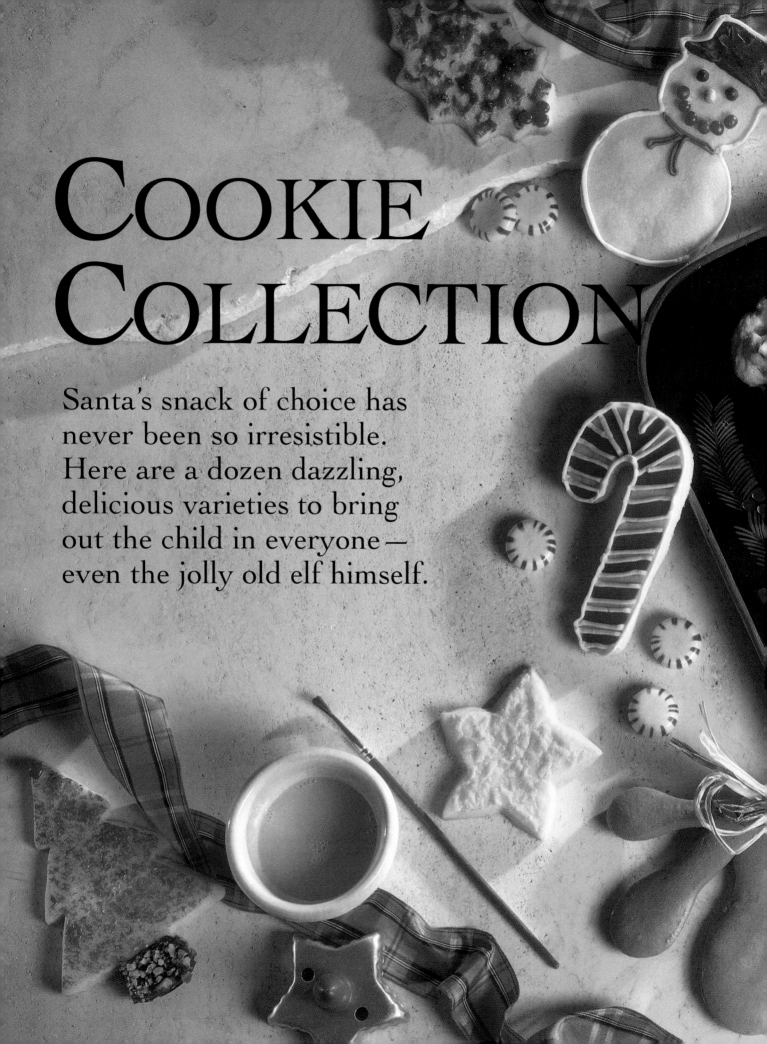

COOKIE COLLECTION

Santa's snack of choice has
never been so irresistible.
Here are a dozen dazzling,
delicious varieties to bring
out the child in everyone—
even the jolly old elf himself.

Royal Rum Balls

Rudolph's Cookies

Ready, Set, Bake
Stir up a jolly holiday with these tasty favorites.

Royal Rum Balls

These colossal treats are a snap to make. And the longer they sit, the better they taste!

2 cups gingersnap crumbs
2 cups chocolate wafer crumbs
1½ cups sifted powdered sugar
1 cup flaked coconut
1 cup ground pecans, toasted
⅓ cup pitted dates, chopped
⅓ cup dark rum
3 tablespoons light corn syrup
2 tablespoons butter or margarine, melted
1 teaspoon vanilla extract
Additional powdered sugar or gingersnap crumbs

Position knife blade in food processor bowl; add first 6 ingredients. Process until blended; add rum and next 3 ingredients. Process until mixture holds together.

Shape into 1¼" balls. Roll balls in additional powdered sugar or gingersnap crumbs. Repeat rolling procedure. **Yield:** 3 dozen.

Note: If Royal Rum Balls are made ahead, reroll balls in powdered sugar or gingersnap crumbs before serving to freshen the coating.

Rudolph's Cookies

Red currant jelly dollops Christmas color on these pecan-coated thumbprint cookies.

1 cup butter, softened
¾ cup sugar
2 large eggs, separated
1 teaspoon almond extract
2 cups all-purpose flour
¼ teaspoon salt
1¼ teaspoons ground cinnamon
1¼ cups finely chopped pecans
Red currant jelly

Beat butter at medium speed of an electric mixer until creamy. Gradually add sugar, beating well. Add egg yolks and almond extract, beating until blended.

Combine flour, salt, and cinnamon. Add flour mixture to butter mixture, blending at low speed. Cover and chill dough 1 hour.

Shape dough into 1" balls. Lightly beat egg whites. Dip each ball in egg white; roll in pecans. Place 2" apart on ungreased cookie sheets. Press thumb in each cookie to make an indentation.

Bake at 350° for 15 minutes. Cool 1 minute on cookie sheets; remove to wire racks to cool completely. Press centers again with thumb while cookies are still warm; fill center of each cookie with jelly. **Yield:** about 3½ dozen.

Peanut Butter Stacks

Caramel-Filled
Chocolate Cookies

Peanut Butter Stacks

Children will enjoy sandwiching peanut butter
cup candies between classic peanut butter cookies.

½ cup butter or margarine, softened
½ cup chunky peanut butter
1 cup firmly packed brown sugar
1 large egg
1 teaspoon vanilla extract
1¼ cups all-purpose flour
½ teaspoon baking soda
½ teaspoon salt
12 (.9-ounce) peanut butter cup candies

Beat butter and peanut butter at medium speed of
an electric mixer until creamy; gradually add sugar,
beating well. Add egg and vanilla; beat well.

Combine flour, soda, and salt; add to butter mixture, beating well. Cover and chill dough 1 hour.

Shape dough into 24 balls; place half of dough balls
2" apart on a lightly greased cookie sheet. Dip a fork
in water and flatten cookies in a crisscross pattern.

Bake at 350° for 10 minutes. Cool slightly on
cookie sheet; transfer to a wire rack. Let cool.

Place remaining dough balls on greased cookie
sheet; repeat crisscross procedure with fork. Bake at
350° for 8 minutes. Let cool slightly; turn cookies
over on cookie sheet, so crisscross pattern is down.
Place a peanut butter cup candy on each cookie.

Bake an additional 2 minutes or until candies
soften. Remove from oven. Top each with a baked
cookie, pressing to form sandwiches. **Yield:** 1 dozen.

Caramel-Filled Chocolate Cookies

Deep inside each chocolaty mound is a surprise
caramel candy filling.

1 cup butter or margarine, softened
1 cup sugar
1 cup firmly packed brown sugar
2 large eggs
2 teaspoons vanilla extract
2¼ cups all-purpose flour
1 teaspoon baking soda
¾ cup cocoa
1 cup finely chopped pecans, divided
1 tablespoon sugar
1 (9-ounce) package chewy caramels in milk
   chocolate

Beat butter at medium speed of an electric mixer
until creamy; gradually add sugars, beating well.
Add eggs and vanilla; beat well.

Combine flour, soda, and cocoa; gradually add to
butter mixture, beating well. Stir in ½ cup pecans.
Cover and chill dough at least 2 hours. Combine
remaining ½ cup pecans and 1 tablespoon sugar.

Divide dough into 4 equal portions. Work with 1
portion at a time, storing remainder in refrigerator.
Divide each portion into 12 pieces. Quickly press
each piece of dough around a caramel; roll into a
ball. Dip one side of ball in pecan mixture. Place
balls, pecan side up, 2" apart on ungreased cookie
sheets.

Bake at 375° for 8 minutes. (Cookies will look
soft.) Let cool 1 minute on cookie sheets; remove to
wire racks and let cool completely. **Yield:** 4 dozen.

Peppermint Crescents

These peppermint-topped buttery crescents will melt in your mouth.

1 cup butter, softened
⅔ cup sifted powdered sugar
1 teaspoon peppermint extract
⅛ teaspoon salt
2½ cups all-purpose flour
2 cups sifted powdered sugar, divided
2½ tablespoons milk
¼ teaspoon peppermint extract
    Coarsely crushed hard peppermint candy

Beat butter at medium speed of an electric mixer until creamy. Add ⅔ cup powdered sugar, 1 teaspoon peppermint extract, and salt; beat well. Gradually add flour to butter mixture, beating at low speed just until blended after each addition. Divide dough into thirds; cover and chill 30 minutes.

Working with 1 portion of dough at a time, divide each portion into 12 pieces. Roll each piece into a 2" log; curve ends of each log to form a crescent. Place crescents 2" apart on lightly greased cookie sheets.

Bake at 325° for 18 minutes or until lightly browned. Cool on cookie sheets 1 minute. Carefully roll warm cookies in 1 cup powdered sugar; let cool completely on wire racks.

Combine remaining 1 cup sugar, milk, and ¼ teaspoon peppermint extract, stirring until smooth. Drizzle icing over cookies and sprinkle with crushed peppermint, pressing gently. Let icing set before serving. Store in an airtight container. **Yield:** 3 dozen.

Cherry Icebox Cookies

Speed the chilling of the dough by placing the rolls in the freezer; then just slice and bake.

1 cup butter, softened
1 cup sugar
1 large egg
1 teaspoon vanilla extract
2¾ cups all-purpose flour
1 teaspoon baking powder
½ teaspoon salt
1 (16-ounce) jar maraschino cherries, drained and finely chopped
1 cup finely chopped pecans
¼ cup red decorator sugar (optional)

Beat butter at medium speed of an electric mixer until creamy. Gradually add 1 cup sugar, beating well. Add egg and vanilla, beating well.

Combine flour, baking powder, and salt; add to butter mixture, beating well. Pat cherries between paper towels to remove excess moisture. Stir cherries and pecans into dough; cover and chill 2 hours.

Shape dough into two 1½"-diameter, 8"-long rolls. Roll in colored sugar, if desired. Wrap rolls in wax paper and freeze until firm.

Unwrap frozen dough and slice into ¼"-thick slices, using a sharp knife. Place on lightly greased cookie sheets.

Bake at 400° for 8 to 10 minutes or until golden. Let cool 1 minute on cookie sheets. Transfer to wire racks to cool completely. **Yield:** 4 dozen.

Costumed Sugar Cookies

Costumed Sugar Cookies

You'll find this the best sugar cookie dough ever. Sponge paint some of these cookies with a sea sponge and egg yolk paint before baking them.

 1 cup butter, softened
1½ cups sugar
 1 large egg
3⅓ cups all-purpose flour
 1 teaspoon cream of tartar
 ½ teaspoon salt
 1 egg yolk, lightly beaten
 ¼ teaspoon water
   Assorted colors of paste food coloring
   Decorator sugar
   Vanilla and chocolate ready-to-spread frosting
   Chocolate candy bar sprinkles (optional)
   Chopped pecans (optional)
   Melted semisweet chocolate (optional)
   Red cinnamon candies (optional)

Beat butter at medium speed of an electric mixer 2 minutes or until creamy. Gradually add 1½ cups sugar, beating well. Add egg and beat well.

Combine flour, cream of tartar, and salt; add to butter mixture, beating at low speed just until blended.

Roll dough to ¼" thickness between 2 sheets of wax paper. Cut with cookie cutters. Place 1" apart on ungreased cookie sheets.

Combine egg yolk and water; stir well. Divide mixture among several cups. Tint with desired colors of food coloring. Keep egg yolk paint covered until ready to use. Add a few drops of water if paint thickens too much.

Using a small paintbrush or sea sponge, paint assorted designs on some cookies with egg yolk paint. Sprinkle some cookies with decorator sugar. (Some cookies will be baked plain.)

Bake at 350° for 10 to 12 minutes. Let cookies stand 1 minute on cookie sheets. Carefully transfer cookies to wire racks to cool completely. Frost remaining cookies with vanilla and chocolate frosting and decorate as desired. **Yield:** 2½ dozen.

Gingerbread Spoons

Gingerbread Spoons

Serve these edible spoons with ice cream, tie several atop a gift, or hang them on the tree.

½ cup butter or margarine, softened
¾ cup firmly packed dark brown sugar
1 large egg
⅓ cup molasses
2½ tablespoons lemon juice
3 to 3½ cups all-purpose flour, divided
1 tablespoon baking powder
¼ teaspoon baking soda
   Dash of salt
1½ teaspoons ground ginger
1 teaspoon ground cinnamon
¼ teaspoon ground cloves
   Uncooked spaghetti

Beat butter at medium speed of an electric mixer until creamy; gradually add brown sugar, beating well. Add egg, molasses, and lemon juice; beat well.

   Combine 1 cup flour and next 6 ingredients; stir well. Add to butter mixture, beating until blended. Gradually add enough remaining flour to make a stiff dough. Cover and chill dough 1 hour.

   Divide dough into 2 portions. Roll each portion on a lightly greased cookie sheet to ¼" thickness; cover and freeze until firm.

   Using real spoons as patterns, trace spoons onto dough with a sharp knife, about 2" apart. Remove excess dough from cookie sheet.

   Repeat procedure with remaining frozen dough. Combine scraps of dough and repeat procedure until all dough is used. To prepare cookies for stringing together, insert a 1" piece of spaghetti into narrow end of each dough cutout.

   Bake at 350° for 10 minutes or until golden. Let cool 1 minute on cookie sheets. Remove to wire racks; remove spaghetti pieces and let cookies cool completely. Thread raffia or string through cookies, if desired. **Yield:** 5 dozen.

Note: Use uncooked spaghetti to prepare cookies for stringing and hanging only. Remove and discard spaghetti pieces while cookies are still warm.

Speckled Shortbread

Vanilla and chocolate flavor this Scottish classic.

½ cup shortening
½ cup butter, softened
1 cup sugar
1 vanilla bean, split lengthwise
1 egg yolk
2 cups all-purpose flour
⅛ teaspoon salt
1 (1-ounce) square semisweet chocolate, grated

Beat shortening and butter at medium speed of an electric mixer until creamy; gradually add sugar, beating until light and fluffy.

   Scrape vanilla bean seeds into mixture; discard pod. Beat in egg yolk. Add flour and salt, beating at low speed just until blended. Stir in grated chocolate. Press dough into an ungreased 15" x 10" x 1" jelly-roll pan.

   Bake at 325° for 25 minutes. Let cool slightly in pan. Cut shortbread into 3" x 1¼" strips, using a fluted pastry wheel. Let cool completely in pan. **Yield:** 3 dozen.

Shortbread Wedges: Press half of dough into an ungreased 9" round cakepan. Bake at 325° for 28 to 30 minutes. Let cool slightly in pan. Cut shortbread into thin wedges. Repeat procedure with remaining dough. **Yield:** 2 dozen.

Chunky Hazelnut-Toffee Cookies

The toffee candy bars and toasted hazelnuts in this chocolate treat demand a cold glass of milk.

   1 cup unsalted butter, softened
   ¾ cup firmly packed brown sugar
   ½ cup sugar
   2 large eggs
   1 tablespoon vanilla extract
   2¾ cups all-purpose flour
   1½ teaspoons baking powder
   ½ teaspoon baking soda
   ½ teaspoon salt
   4 (1.4-ounce) English toffee-flavored candy
      bars, chopped
   2 (10-ounce) packages semisweet chocolate
      chunks
   1 cup toasted, chopped hazelnuts or pecans

Beat butter at medium speed of an electric mixer until creamy. Gradually add sugars, beating well. Add eggs and vanilla, beating well.

   Combine flour and next 3 ingredients, stirring well. Add to butter mixture, beating at low speed just until blended. Stir in candy bars, chocolate, and nuts. Drop dough by heaping tablespoonfuls 1½" apart onto ungreased cookie sheets.

   Bake at 350° for 10 minutes or until lightly browned. Let cool slightly on cookie sheets; remove to wire racks and let cool completely. **Yield:** 4½ dozen.

Amaretti Triple Deckers

Graham crackers, chocolate wafers, and white frosting provide three layers of color and flavor.

   1 cup butter or margarine, melted
   ½ cup sugar
   1½ teaspoons vanilla extract
   ¼ teaspoon salt
   2 large eggs, lightly beaten
   2 cups chocolate wafer crumbs
   ¾ cup slivered almonds, toasted and chopped
   ½ cup flaked coconut
   1¼ cups graham cracker crumbs
   ½ cup finely crushed amaretti cookies
   ½ cup semisweet chocolate mini-morsels
   ¼ cup butter or margarine, softened
   2¾ cups sifted powdered sugar
   2 tablespoons milk
   ¼ teaspoon almond extract
   1 (1-ounce) square semisweet chocolate, melted
   20 amarettini cookies (miniature amaretti
      cookies)

Combine first 5 ingredients in a heavy saucepan. Cook over medium-low heat, stirring constantly with a wire whisk, 12 to 15 minutes or until mixture reaches 160° and is slightly thickened. Remove from heat; divide mixture in half. Let cool 15 minutes.

   Add chocolate wafer crumbs, almonds, and coconut to half of butter mixture, stirring well.

Press chocolate mixture firmly into an ungreased 9" square pan.

Add graham cracker crumbs, crushed amaretti cookies, and chocolate mini-morsels to remaining mixture, stirring well. Press graham cracker mixture firmly over chocolate mixture in pan.

Beat ¼ cup butter at medium speed of an electric mixer until creamy; gradually add powdered sugar, beating until blended. Add milk and almond extract; beat until mixture is spreading consistency. Spread frosting over graham cracker layer. Cover and chill. Cut into 20 bars.

Spoon melted chocolate into a zip-top plastic bag. Snip a tiny hole in one corner of bag, using scissors. Drizzle chocolate over frosted bars. Top each bar with an amarettini cookie. **Yield:** 20 bars.

Café au Lait Squares

Café au Lait Squares

Coffee lovers will swoon over these moist brownies dotted with chocolate coffee beans.

1¼ cups all-purpose flour, divided
 1 cup quick-cooking oats, uncooked
 ½ cup firmly packed brown sugar
 ⅓ cup butter or margarine, melted
 1 tablespoon instant coffee granules
 ¼ teaspoon salt
 ⅓ cup butter or margarine
 2 (1-ounce) squares unsweetened chocolate
 2 large eggs
 1 cup sugar
 2 tablespoons Kahlúa or other coffee-flavored liqueur
¾ cup toasted, chopped walnuts
 Coffee Frosting
 Chocolate coffee beans (optional)

Combine ½ cup flour, oats, and next 4 ingredients; stir well. Press flour mixture into an ungreased 9" square pan. Bake at 350° for 12 minutes.

Combine ⅓ cup butter and chocolate in a small saucepan. Cook over medium-low heat until melted, stirring frequently. Let cool.

Beat eggs at medium speed of an electric mixer until thick and pale. Add 1 cup sugar and Kahlúa, beating until blended. Stir in chocolate mixture, remaining ¾ cup flour, and walnuts; spread mixture evenly over crust.

Bake at 350° for 25 minutes. Cool in pan on a wire rack. Spread Coffee Frosting over brownies. Cover and let stand until frosting hardens. Cut into 16 squares. Garnish with chocolate coffee beans, if desired. **Yield:** 16 squares.

Coffee Frosting

 ⅓ cup butter or margarine, softened
2¼ cups sifted powdered sugar
1½ tablespoons Kahlúa or other coffee-flavored liqueur
 2 tablespoons finely chopped chocolate coffee beans

Beat butter at medium speed of an electric mixer until creamy. Gradually add sugar and Kahlúa, beating until blended. Fold in chopped coffee beans. **Yield:** 1 cup.

Note: Chocolate coffee beans are available at specialty food shops or gourmet candy counters. Substitute cold brewed coffee for Kahlúa, if desired.

Sweet Tooth
Truffle Tree

CHOCOLATE GALORE

What would a Christmas fete be without everyone's favorite indulgence? In honor of the season, chocolate takes some delectable turns—truffle trees, fudgy brownies, and darkly glazed pound cakes.

Deep Dark Brownie Diamonds

The Sweetest Endings Begin with Chocolate

Any one of our eight fabulous finishes will polish off your holiday dinner in the best of taste.

Deep Dark Brownie Diamonds

Chocolate-raspberry morsels add a hint of berry flavor to these incredibly rich brownies. Substitute regular semisweet morsels, if desired.

 3 cups (18 ounces) semisweet chocolate morsels
1½ cups firmly packed brown sugar
 1 cup unsalted butter
 4 large eggs, lightly beaten
1½ cups all-purpose flour
 1 tablespoon instant coffee granules
 ¼ teaspoon salt
 1 tablespoon vanilla extract
 ¾ cup whipping cream
1¼ cups (8 ounces) semisweet
   chocolate-raspberry morsels
1½ tablespoons unsalted butter
 ½ teaspoon almond extract
   Crystallized violets (optional)

Line a 13" x 9" x 2" pan with aluminum foil, allowing foil to extend over narrow ends of pan. Grease foil and set aside.

Combine first 3 ingredients in a heavy saucepan. Cook over medium heat until chocolate and butter melt, stirring often. Remove from heat and let cool slightly. Gradually stir about ¼ of hot mixture into beaten eggs; add to remaining hot mixture, beating well at low speed of an electric mixer.

Combine flour, coffee granules, and salt; add to chocolate mixture, beating just until blended. Stir in vanilla. Pour batter into prepared pan.

Bake at 350° for 28 minutes. (Do not overbake.) Let cool completely in pan on a wire rack.

Lift foil out of pan; invert brownies onto a cutting board. Remove foil, leaving brownies smooth side up. Trim outer edges to form a 12" x 8" brownie rectangle. Cut crosswise into 8 (1½") strips. Trim a thin diagonal slice from both ends of each strip. (Reserve brownie scraps for another use, if desired.)

Cut each strip diagonally into 4 diamonds. Place brownie diamonds 2" apart on wire racks over a jellyroll pan lined with wax paper.

Bring whipping cream to a simmer over medium heat in a heavy saucepan. Remove from heat; add chocolate-raspberry morsels, 1½ tablespoons butter, and almond extract. Let stand 1 minute. Stir gently until chocolate melts completely. Let glaze cool slightly.

Pour glaze over brownie diamonds, completely covering tops and sides. Spoon up excess glaze. Continue coating until all brownies have been glazed. Let brownies stand at room temperature until glaze is set. Top each with a violet, if desired. **Yield:** 32 brownies.

Note: Brownies may be covered and stored in refrigerator up to 3 days before serving. Let stand 20 minutes at room temperature before serving.

Cut each brownie strip diagonally into four diamonds. Place 2" apart on wire racks.

Sweet Tooth Truffle Tree

Display this fanciful tree as an edible centerpiece. For a quick alternative, buy commercial truffles and top the tree with a star ornament or fabric bow.

  2 cups whipping cream
2½ tablespoons instant coffee granules
  2 pounds semisweet chocolate, finely chopped
      Coatings: finely chopped pistachio nuts, ground almonds or pecans, chocolate sprinkles, cocoa, flaked coconut, nonpareils, crushed hard red and green peppermint candies, red and green sprinkles
  1 (10") Styrofoam cone
      Cocoa
      Dark Chocolate Bow

Combine whipping cream and coffee granules in a large saucepan; bring to a simmer over medium heat. Remove from heat and add chopped chocolate; let stand 3 minutes. Stir gently until chocolate melts completely.

Pour mixture into an ungreased 13" x 9" x 2" pan. Let cool to room temperature (about 1 hour). Cover and chill 1½ hours or until firm.

Shape mixture into 1¼" balls, using a small cookie scoop. Place balls on a wax paper-lined jelly-roll pan. Cover and chill until firm.

Roll balls in desired coatings. Lightly dust foam cone with cocoa, coating completely. Using small wooden picks, attach truffles to cone, one at a time, starting at base of cone and working in circular rows, covering cone completely.

Attach Dark Chocolate Bow strips with a wooden pick to top of tree; top with assembled Dark Chocolate Bow. Cover and chill until ready to serve. Use small tongs to remove truffles from tree, if desired. **Yield:** about 5 dozen truffles.

Dark Chocolate Bow
  8 ounces dark sweet chocolate, finely chopped
¼ cup light corn syrup

Place half of chocolate in top of a double boiler over hot water; stir with a rubber spatula until chocolate melts. Add remaining half of chocolate, stirring until chocolate melts. Stir in corn syrup; remove from heat

and let cool slightly. Remove and set aside 2 tablespoons chocolate mixture. Spread remaining chocolate mixture to ⅓" thickness on wax paper-lined cookie sheet. Chill 20 minutes or just until firm.

Feed firm chocolate slab through smooth roller of a cold pasta machine set on 2. Immediately cut chocolate into ¾"-wide strips. Cut strips into 5" and 7" segments. Fold 5" segments to form loops, pressing ends gently together. Drape 7" segments over empty egg cartons, creating a wavy appearance.

Make a bow with chocolate loops, overlapping loops on a wooden pick; use 2 tablespoons reserved chocolate mixture as "glue" between layers. Chill strips and bow until firm. **Yield:** enough for 1 Dark Chocolate Bow.

Note: If you don't have a pasta machine, spread chocolate mixture to about ⅛" thickness on a large marble slab. Let harden and cut into strips, using a sharp knife.

Carefully insert wooden picks into foam cone, about 1½" apart. Attach truffles.

Almond Macaroon Tart

You'll think you're eating a candy bar when you take the first bite of this dessert laden with coconut, almonds, and chocolate.

1¼ cups chocolate wafer crumbs
  1 cup sliced almonds, ground
  ¼ cup butter or margarine, melted
  2 egg whites
  ⅓ cup sugar
  1 (7-ounce) package flaked coconut
  ⅓ cup sweetened condensed milk
  1 teaspoon vanilla extract
  ¼ cup butter or margarine
  3 (1-ounce) squares unsweetened
     chocolate, chopped
  3 large eggs
  ½ cup sugar
  ⅛ teaspoon salt
  1 teaspoon vanilla extract
  1 cup whole natural almonds
 10 (1-ounce) squares semisweet chocolate, divided
  ½ cup whipping cream
  1 tablespoon light corn syrup
  1 ounce white chocolate, chopped
1½ teaspoons shortening

Combine first 3 ingredients in a bowl, stirring well. Pat mixture onto bottom and sides of a lightly greased 11" tart pan. Bake at 350° for 10 minutes.

Beat egg whites at high speed of an electric mixer until soft peaks form. Gradually add ⅓ cup sugar, beating 4 minutes or until thickened. Stir in coconut, sweetened condensed milk, and 1 teaspoon vanilla. Spread coconut mixture over crust in pan.

Melt ¼ cup butter and unsweetened chocolate in a heavy saucepan over medium-low heat. Remove from heat.

Beat 3 eggs at medium speed until thick and frothy. Gradually add ½ cup sugar, salt, and 1 teaspoon vanilla, beating until blended. Stir in melted chocolate mixture. Spoon over coconut mixture in tart pan.

Bake at 350° for 40 minutes. Let cool completely; carefully remove sides of tart pan.

Roast whole almonds on a baking sheet at 350° for 8 to 12 minutes. Let cool. Melt 4 ounces semisweet chocolate in top of a double boiler over hot,

not simmering, water. Remove from heat and let cool until chocolate registers 90° on an instant-read thermometer. Add roasted almonds, stirring constantly for 2 to 3 minutes until chocolate begins to set. Remove chocolate-coated almonds and let dry on wax paper.

Bring whipping cream and corn syrup to a boil in a small saucepan. Remove from heat and pour over remaining 6 ounces semisweet chocolate. Let stand 1 minute. Whisk until smooth. Pour chocolate mixture over baked tart. Place chocolate-coated almonds around edge of tart.

Melt white chocolate and shortening in top of double boiler over hot, not simmering, water. Remove from heat and drizzle over tart. Let stand until topping is set. **Yield:** one 11" tart.

Black Bottom Mocha Pie

This classic chocolate pie with its nutty crust needs only a simple garnish of whipped cream and chocolate shavings.

  ½ cup pecan pieces
1½ cups all-purpose flour
  ½ cup butter or margarine
2½ tablespoons orange juice
  1 (6-ounce) package semisweet chocolate
     morsels
  1 (5-ounce) can evaporated milk
  2 tablespoons brown sugar
  1 tablespoon butter or margarine
  ½ teaspoon vanilla or rum extract
  1 envelope unflavored gelatin
1¼ cups chocolate milk, divided
  ⅓ cup sugar
  1 tablespoon instant coffee granules
  2 egg yolks, lightly beaten
  2 cups frozen whipped topping, thawed
     Garnishes: whipped topping, chocolate
     shavings

Position knife blade in food processor bowl; add pecan pieces and process until pecans are coarsely chopped. Add flour.

Drop ½ cup butter, 1 tablespoon at a time, through food chute with processor running; process until mixture is crumbly. Pour orange juice through

Almond Macaroon Tart

food chute; process 1 minute or until dough forms a ball. Remove dough; cover and chill 1 to 2 hours.

Roll dough to a 12" circle between 2 sheets of wax paper. Remove top piece of wax paper and invert dough into a 9" pieplate; remove remaining wax paper. Trim edges of crust; prick bottom and sides of dough with a fork. Bake at 350° for 20 to 25 minutes or until lightly browned. Let cool.

Combine chocolate morsels and next 3 ingredients in a small saucepan. Cook over low heat until chocolate and butter melt, stirring often. Remove from heat; stir in vanilla. Spoon chocolate mixture into prepared crust.

Sprinkle gelatin over ½ cup chocolate milk in a saucepan; let stand 1 minute. Stir in remaining ¾ cup chocolate milk, ⅓ cup sugar, and coffee granules. Cook over low heat 2 minutes, stirring until gelatin and coffee granules dissolve.

Gradually stir about ¼ of hot mixture into egg yolks; add to remaining hot mixture, stirring constantly. Cook 1 minute or until mixture reaches 160° (do not boil). Remove from heat; chill 30 minutes or until consistency of unbeaten egg white.

Fold 2 cups whipped topping into gelatin mixture; spoon into crust over chocolate layer. Cover and chill until firm. Garnish, if desired. **Yield:** one 9" pie.

Frozen Cocoa-Mint Crêpes

A frozen crêpe filled with minted whipped cream provides a doubly cool taste sensation.

⅔ cup all-purpose flour
2 tablespoons sugar
1 tablespoon cocoa
¾ cup plus 2 tablespoons milk
1 large egg
2 teaspoons vegetable oil
  Vegetable oil
2 (4.67-ounce) packages chocolate-covered mint wafer candies, divided
2½ cups whipping cream
¼ cup sifted powdered sugar
¼ cup whipping cream
1 tablespoon light corn syrup
  Garnishes: fresh mint sprigs, chocolate shavings

Combine first 4 ingredients, beating with a wire whisk until smooth. Add egg and beat well; stir in 2 teaspoons oil. Chill batter at least 2 hours.

Coat bottom of a 6" crêpe pan or heavy skillet with oil; place over medium heat until hot.

Pour 2 tablespoons batter into pan; quickly tilt pan in all directions so batter covers bottom of pan. Cook 1 minute or until crêpe can be shaken loose from pan. Turn crêpe over and cook about 30 seconds. Place crêpe on a dish towel to cool. Repeat with remaining batter. Stack crêpes between sheets of wax paper to prevent sticking.

Unwrap and chop 1 package of chocolate mint candies. Beat 2½ cups whipping cream and powdered sugar at high speed of an electric mixer until stiff peaks form. Gently fold in chopped mint candies. Cover and freeze 5 minutes.

Spoon ⅓ cup whipped cream mixture in center of each crêpe. Fold left and right side of each crêpe toward center. Place, seam side down, in a dish and freeze at least 2 hours.

Combine remaining chocolate mint candies, ¼ cup whipping cream, and corn syrup in a saucepan. Cook over medium-low heat until chocolate melts, stirring often. Remove from heat; let cool slightly.

Place 2 crêpes on each serving plate. Drizzle warm sauce over crêpes. Garnish, if desired.
Yield: 6 servings.

Chocolate Linzertorte

This elegant torte, which originated in Linz, Austria, boasts a raspberry jam filling encased in a buttery chocolate-almond lattice crust.

¾ cup butter, softened
½ cup sugar
3 egg yolks
2 cups all-purpose flour
¼ teaspoon salt
1 teaspoon ground allspice
3 (1-ounce) squares semisweet chocolate, melted and cooled
1½ cups whole natural almonds, toasted and ground
  Vegetable cooking spray
1 cup seedless raspberry jam
1 (6-ounce) package semisweet chocolate morsels
½ cup whipping cream, whipped

Beat butter at medium speed of an electric mixer until soft and creamy; gradually add sugar, beating well. Add egg yolks, beating well.

Combine flour, salt, and allspice; add to butter mixture alternately with melted chocolate, beginning and ending with flour mixture. Stir in almonds. Divide dough in half.

Roll half of dough between 2 sheets of wax paper to an 11" circle. Freeze 15 minutes. Press remaining half of dough into an 11" tart pan coated with cooking spray.

Bake at 375° for 5 minutes. Stir jam well and spread over crust. Sprinkle with chocolate morsels.

Remove top sheet of wax paper from frozen circle of dough; cut into ½"-wide strips, using a fluted pastry wheel. Arrange strips in lattice design over torte, sealing ends of strips to prebaked crust.

Bake at 375° for 20 to 25 minutes. Let cool completely in pan on a wire rack. Serve torte at room temperature with whipped cream.
Yield: one 11" torte.

Chocolate Linzertorte

Mississippi Mud Brûlée

These individual chocolate custards are topped with gooey marshmallow and a caramelized sugar crust—reminiscent of a s'more.

    2 cups whipping cream
  ⅓ cup sugar
    6 egg yolks, lightly beaten
    1 (4-ounce) bar sweet baking chocolate, melted
  ¼ cup Kahlúa or other coffee-flavored liqueur
  ⅓ cup marshmallow cream
1½ tablespoons semisweet chocolate mini-morsels
  ¾ teaspoon milk
  ½ cup loosely packed brown sugar

Combine whipping cream and ⅓ cup sugar in a small heavy saucepan; bring to a simmer (do not boil). Remove from heat and gradually stir about ¼ of hot mixture into yolks; add to remaining hot mixture, stirring constantly. Stir in melted sweet chocolate and Kahlúa.

Pour chocolate mixture into 6 (6-ounce) ungreased ramekins. Place ramekins in a 13" x 9" x 2" pan. Add hot water to pan to depth of 1". Bake, uncovered, at 300° for 30 to 40 minutes or just until set. Remove ramekins from pan and let cool on a wire rack. Cover and chill thoroughly.

Combine marshmallow cream, mini-morsels, and milk, stirring until blended. Spoon a small dollop of marshmallow mixture evenly onto each custard.

Sprinkle brown sugar over marshmallow layer. Place ramekins in a 13" x 9" x 2" pan; fill pan with ice cubes, surrounding ramekins.

Broil 3½" from heat (with electric oven door partially opened) 1 to 2 minutes or until brown sugar melts. Remove ramekins from pan. Chill custards 5 minutes or just until brown sugar forms a crust.
Yield: 6 servings.

Note: Ice cubes keep the custard cold while allowing the brown sugar to melt under heat.

White Ripple Fudge Pound Cake

A cream cheese layer creates a ribbon as it bakes in the center of this fudge-frosted pound cake.

   1 cup butter or margarine, softened
   3 cups sugar
   5 large eggs
2¾ cups sifted cake flour
   ½ teaspoon baking powder
   ¼ teaspoon salt
   ⅓ cup cocoa
   1 cup evaporated milk
   2 (1-ounce) squares unsweetened
      chocolate, melted
   1 teaspoon vanilla extract
   1 (8-ounce) package cream cheese,
      softened
   ¼ cup sugar
   1 large egg
   1 tablespoon cornstarch
      Fudge Frosting

Beat butter at medium speed of an electric mixer until creamy. Gradually add 3 cups sugar, beating at medium speed 5 to 7 minutes. Add 5 eggs, one at a time, beating just until yellow disappears.

Combine flour and next 3 ingredients; add to butter mixture alternately with milk, beginning and ending with flour mixture. Mix at low speed just until blended after each addition. Stir in melted chocolate and vanilla. Set batter aside.

Beat cream cheese at medium speed until smooth. Add ¼ cup sugar, beating well. Add 1 egg and cornstarch, beating until smooth. Pour half of chocolate batter into a greased and floured 10" tube pan; spoon cream cheese batter over chocolate batter, leaving a border around outer edge. Spoon remaining chocolate batter over cream cheese layer.

Bake at 325° for 1 hour and 40 minutes or until a wooden pick inserted in center comes out almost clean. (Do not overbake.) Cool in pan on a wire rack 30 minutes; remove from pan and let cool completely inverted on wire rack. Pour Fudge Frosting over top of cake. **Yield:** one 10" cake.

Fudge Frosting

   1 cup sugar
   ⅓ cup butter or margarine
   ⅓ cup evaporated milk
   ½ cup semisweet chocolate morsels

Combine first 3 ingredients in a small heavy saucepan. Bring to a boil over medium heat. Boil 1 minute, stirring frequently. Remove from heat; add chocolate morsels, stirring until chocolate melts. Place saucepan in a bowl of ice; beat frosting with a wooden spoon 3 to 4 minutes or until thickened and spreading consistency. **Yield:** 1¼ cups.

GLORIOUS GIFTS

Presents you make by hand are always the most special. This brightly colored blanket and pillow set certainly will be warmly received.

A Colorful Finish

This blanket-stitched edging is simple to do and adds crisp detailing. While we did our stitching in red—to contrast with the yellow and the purple—you may choose any three colors that will suit your recipient's decor.

Our cozy polar fleece blanket and pillow gift set is sure to ward off the brisk chill of winter, and the bold colors will look great not only at Christmas but all season long.

Polar Fleece Blanket

You will need:
1¾ yards 60"-wide yellow polar fleece
⅛ yard 60"-wide purple polar fleece
50 yards thick red pearl cotton
darning needle
liquid ravel preventer

Note: Finished size of blanket is 60" square. For polar fleece, see Sources on page 156.

1. Wash and dry fabric. From yellow fleece, cut a 60" square.

2. Using pearl cotton and darning needle and referring to Diagram, blanket-stitch around cut edges of square, with stitches ½" long and ⅜" apart. Hide knots on wrong side of blanket. Apply liquid ravel preventer to knots.

TIP: To keep blanket stitches even, using contrasting color sewing thread, first baste a line ½" from raw edges of blanket. Sew blanket stitches up to line. Remove basting when finished.

3. From purple fleece, cut 4 (3½"-diameter) circles. Blanket-stitch as above around edge of 1 circle, using 36" length of pearl cotton. Repeat for remaining circles.

4. From remaining pearl cotton, cut 3 (10") lengths. Using 1 length of cotton, stitch center of 1 blanket-stitched circle to blanket, 5" from 1 corner. Leave long tails of thread on top; do not tie off thread. Referring to photo, repeat with remaining lengths of pearl cotton on circle; holding all 3 strands as 1, tie a tight knot. Trim tails to 1½". Apply liquid ravel preventer to thread ends. Repeat for remaining circles.

Blanket Stitch

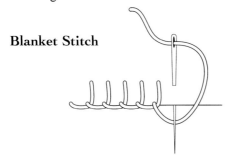

Polar Fleece Pillow

You will need:
⅓ yard 60"-wide red polar fleece
⅓ yard 60"-wide yellow polar fleece
red sewing thread
polyester stuffing
5"-long upholstery needle
4" x 8" piece purple polar fleece
8 yards thick red pearl cotton
darning needle
liquid ravel preventer

Note: Finished size of pillow is 23" square. Seam allowances are ¼". For polar fleece, see Sources on page 156.

1. From red and yellow fleece, cut 4 (12") squares.

2. With right sides facing and raw edges aligned, stitch 1 red square to 1 yellow square along 1 edge. Press seam open. Repeat with remaining squares.

3. With right sides facing, raw edges aligned, and colors alternating side by side (see photo on page 91), stitch 2 red/yellow units together along 1 long edge. Repeat with remaining red/yellow units.

4. With right sides facing, raw edges aligned, and colors alternating, stitch 4-square units together, rounding corners slightly and leaving a 5" opening for turning. Clip corners and turn.

5. Stuff pillow firmly with polyester stuffing. Slipstitch opening closed.

6. Thread upholstery needle with doubled sewing thread. Stitch through center of pillow from front to back several times, pulling thread tightly to create an indention. Tie off thread.

7. From purple fleece, cut 2 (3½"-diameter) circles. Using 36" length of pearl cotton and darning needle, blanket-stitch around edge of each circle as in Step 3 for blanket. Center 1 blanket-stitched circle on each side of pillow and pin in place.

8. Cut 6 (12") lengths of pearl cotton. Using 1 length of cotton, stitch through center of 1 circle to other side of pillow, exiting in center of other circle. Remove needle and adjust thread so that tails are equal in length on each side of pillow. Repeat with remaining lengths of pearl cotton. On 1 side of pillow, divide strands into 2 groups of 3 and tie groups together in knot. Trim tails to 1½". Apply liquid ravel preventer to thread ends. Repeat for other side.

Christmas Card Collages

Fashion these cheerful greeting cards from scraps of papers, fabrics, and laces.

Artist Peggy Gignoux of Chapel Hill, North Carolina, uses everything from sheet music to old photographs to citrus fruit mesh bags for her inspired compositions.

You will need (for 3 cards):
sewing machine with contrasting colors of thread in needle and bobbin (black for needle, red for bobbin shown here)
assorted materials: construction paper, handmade art paper, wrapping paper, marbleized paper, citrus fruit mesh bags, lace, ribbon, fabrics, sheet music
3 (5" x 7") off-white blank greeting cards or cards made from heavyweight card stock (Strathmore cards used here; available from art supply stores)
stick glue (optional)
5" x 7" piece watercolor paper (for star card)

Peggy Gignoux began making her collage cards as a way to use her overflowing collection of scraps left over from her work as a fiber artist. "I never tire of stitching random scraps and odd details into a vibrant whole," she says. For a special touch, Peggy personalizes each card with remnants that relate to her friends' lives.

1. Adjust tension in sewing machine so that bobbin thread shows on top as you stitch. Practice on scrap paper before beginning project.

2. For **tree card**, from green paper, tear 6 wavy strips, decreasing in length from 6" to 2"; also tear 1"-tall triangle. From various colors of paper or fabric, tear or cut 6 wavy strips decreasing in length from 5½" to 1½". From dark ribbon or fabric, cut a small rectangle for tree trunk.

3. Referring to photo, position strips on front of card to make tree shape. Position triangle at top of tree and trunk at bottom. Tear any ragged edges, if necessary. If desired, use stick glue to hold pieces in place. Beginning at bottom corner of tree, stitch back and forth across tree to secure all pieces.

4. For **house card**, from desired materials, tear or cut following pieces for house: 4" square for body, 1½" rectangle for door, 1 (1") and 1 (1¼") square for window, 4½"-tall triangle for roof, small rectangle for chimney, and small circle for doorknob.

5. Referring to photo, position pieces on front of card, gluing if desired. Stitch around perimeter of each shape to secure all pieces.

6. For **star card**, on 5" x 7" piece of watercolor paper, place desired scraps of fabrics, ribbons, and papers to cover entire surface, gluing if desired. Stitch materials in random crisscrossing lines. From scrap piece of paper, cut out star pattern no larger than 5" x 7". Place pattern on top of collaged fabric and cut out star. Center collage star on front of card and stitch around edges to secure.

Star Bowl

Wrapping Paper Bowl

Papier-mâché Panache

It's hard to believe, but the five fabulous creations seen on this page and the next all started with a kitchen mixing bowl and brown paper bags. With papier-mâché, it's that simple to create inexpensive gifts with gallery appeal.

Papier-mâché is the perfect craft for the environmentalist at heart. By recycling brown paper grocery bags, you can create beautiful decorative items for your home and for gifts.

A bowl is one of the simplest papier-mâché projects to master. Follow the step-by-step instructions on page 99; they make this project fun even if this is your first venture.

Papier-mâché Basics

Any kind of paper can be used with papier-mâché, but brown paper bags provide a sturdy base that is easy to make. Always tear the paper for the base; this will give your finished item a smoother surface.

You can use any type of container for your mold, such as a cereal bowl, a platter, or a mixing bowl. Look for items with interesting shapes.

Use a vinyl wallcovering adhesive (found in powdered form at paint and wallpaper stores) to make the paste. (Leftover paste can be stored in an airtight container for up to 4 months.) Once you have completed the layers of your bowl, let the bowl dry completely (drying time will vary with the humidity).

Finish the bowl with one of the following applications. If desired, seal it with a nonyellowing acrylic glaze spray varnish.

Star Bowl

Tear sheets of yellow construction paper into strips as described on page 99. Saturate the strips with paste and cover the inside and the outside of the base bowl completely. For a smooth edge on the bowl, extend the strips over the lip and press them to the back. Transfer the star pattern (see page 148) to the blue construction paper and tear out the stars. Using paste, randomly apply the stars to the inside and the outside of the bowl. Let dry. Apply 2 coats of spray varnish to the bowl, letting dry between applications.

Wrapping Paper Bowl

Tear pieces of last year's Christmas wrapping paper into small pieces. Saturate the pieces with paste and cover the inside and the outside of the base bowl completely. If desired, tear interesting motifs from the paper and adhere them to the inside of the bowl with paste. Apply 2 coats of spray varnish to the bowl, letting dry between applications.

Gilded Bowl

Rose Petal Bowl

Painted Bowl

Rose Petal Bowl

Tear pieces of natural handmade paper (available from art supply stores; or see Sources on page 156) into strips as for the base. Saturate the strips with paste and cover the inside and the outside of the base bowl completely. (Since handmade paper is so fibrous, it may take a couple of layers to hide the brown paper.) Let dry.

Position loose red rose petals randomly around the inside and the outside of the bowl; then cover each with 1 small torn piece of handmade paper saturated with paste. The appearance of the petals will be subtle.

Gilded Bowl

Tear pieces of packing paper (see lower right corner of photo above) into small pieces. Saturate the paper with paste and cover the inside of the base bowl. Let dry. Referring to the manufacturer's directions, randomly apply gold leaf (see Sources on page 156) to the inside and the outside of the bowl. Let dry.

Painted Bowl

Using acrylic paints, paint the inside of the base bowl red and the outside green. Let dry and then repeat.

Transfer the leaf pattern (see page 153) randomly to the inside and the outside of the bowl. Paint the inside leaves green and the outside leaves red. Let dry. Referring to the photo and using cream acrylic paint, add dots along the leaves. Apply 2 coats of spray varnish to the bowl, letting dry between applications.

Papier-mâché Made Easy

You will need:
metal or glass bowl for mold
petroleum jelly
plastic wrap
large disposable bowl for mixing adhesive
powdered vinyl wallcovering adhesive
brown paper grocery bags, torn into ½"- to
   1"-wide, 5"- to 7"-long strips
assorted paints, papers, and foil for finishing
   (See pages 97 and 98.)

1. Coat bowl to be covered with a thin layer of petroleum jelly. Press 1 layer of plastic wrap into bowl, covering inside of bowl completely and letting wrap extend 2" over edge of bowl. Smooth out wrinkles as much as possible.

2. Following manufacturer's instructions, add water to wallcovering adhesive to make approximately 2 cups of paste (this will provide enough paste to make 2 to 3 bowls, depending on sizes of bowls). Mixture will appear watery at first but will turn to paste-like consistency in 5 to 10 minutes. Dip 1 torn paper strip into paste to saturate, removing excess paste from strip with fingers. Press strip smoothly into bottom of bowl. Continue adding strips in 1 direction to cover inside of bowl with 1 layer of strips. To form lip on your bowl, let edge of strips extend 1" beyond lip of bowl. (If no lip is desired, stop edges of strips at top edge of bowl.)

3. Once 1 layer has been placed in bowl, begin to place next layer of paste-saturated strips perpendicular to first layer. If lip is desired, position strips to extend straight out from bowl (see photo) by gently molding with your fingers. Let first 2 layers dry for approximately 15 minutes.

4. Continue adding layers for total of 5 to 6 layers for sturdy base. If lip becomes too heavy, prop it up with crumpled aluminum foil.

Let bowl dry completely, overnight at room temperature or in warm oven (lowest setting) for several hours. Once papier-mâché bowl is dry, it will easily lift out of mixing bowl. Discard plastic wrap and wash mixing bowl thoroughly for future use.

Heidi King, of Tallahassee, Florida, created the five bowls featured here. "I love papier-mâché because of the possibilities in design and also because it's so inexpensive," she says.

Old-fashioned Handkerchief Sachet

Craft this sweet pillow from a vintage handkerchief and fill it with aromatic potpourri. Hanging on a bedside table, it will sweeten dreams with delicate fragrance.

You will need:
1 (10"-square) white handkerchief
thread to match handkerchief
gold metallic sewing thread
26 (3-mm) pearl beads
1 large decorative pearl button
1¼ yards ⅞"-wide white wire-edged ribbon with gold edging
12" length ¾"-wide white organza ribbon with gold edging
¼ yard muslin
2 tablespoons potpourri
polyester stuffing

Note: Finished size of sachet is approximately 6½" square. Antique handkerchiefs are often available at flea markets, tag sales, and antique shops.

1. Referring to photo, with wrong sides facing, fold sides and bottom of handkerchief to center to form an envelope. Blindstitch edges to secure, leaving top flap free.

Whipstitch with Beads

2. Referring to photo and Diagram and using gold thread, whipstitch 13 pearl beads each along edges of top and bottom flaps of sachet.

3. Using gold thread, stitch button to point of top flap.

4. For handle, cut 12" from wired ribbon. Turn ends of ribbon under and handstitch ends to top corners of sachet at back. From remaining wired ribbon, make double-loop bow and tack to center of handle. Tie organza ribbon around center of bow.

5. From muslin, cut 2 (6") squares or size needed to fit inside sachet. With right sides facing and raw edges aligned, stitch pieces together, leaving an opening for turning. Turn. Fill with potpourri and stuffing. Stitch opening closed. Insert pouch into sachet and close top flap.

Say It with Flowers

It's all in the phrasing with tussie-mussies, those lovely nosegays made from flowers whose messages mean as much as their beauty.

Victorian women literally wore their feelings on their sleeves when they pinned on a tussie-mussie. The flowers signified love, luck, and a host of other wishes (see page 104).

Nowadays, let the petite bouquets spread your Christmas message in one of the delightful ways pictured here. For most of the materials used in these tussie-mussies, see Sources on page 156.

Christmas Tussie-mussie

102

Place Favor Tussie-mussie

For a holiday dinner guest, make this miniature **place favor** tussie-mussie from roses, alstroemeria, strawflowers, rosemary, and pine.

Mistletoe Tussie-mussie

Branches of mistletoe and ivy encircle three white roses in this **mistletoe** tussie-mussie, shown hanging elegantly from an overhead light.

Holiday Everlasting Tussie-mussie

The **holiday everlasting** tussie-mussie, made of cherry red roses, statice, poppy pods, hemlock cones, rosemary, ivy, pine, and cinnamon sticks, will dry beautifully when hung upside down.

Create Your Own Tussie-mussies

Geraldine Laufer, a noted horticulturist and author, interprets the fragrant language of flowers through her own charming designs.

Geraldine's advice to wear comfortable shoes was greatly appreciated as we wandered across Frog Holler, her home and site of her glorious garden—a paradise of rolling hills covered with native azalea, wild hydrangea, and camellia; a pond scattered with water lilies; and a formal herb garden.

Geraldine uses materials from her garden to make her floral creations and supplements her harvest with flowers from the local farmer's market. Here, Geraldine shows you in clear, step-by-step detail how to make the tussie-mussie shown on page 102 and above. Use these same instructions to fashion tussie-mussies from any flowers you choose.

You will need:
desired floral, herbal, and greenery materials (3 red roses, 6 red/white miniature carnations, variegated holly and berries, baby's breath, parsley, peppermint, rosemary, and large ivy leaves used here)
garden scissors
florist's tape
lace collar or paper doily (See Step 6.)
1 yard desired ribbon
posy holder (optional)

Note: Pretreat natural materials by cutting stems on diagonal. Remove lower leaves from stems and plunge them into tepid water with floral preservative added. Let them sit overnight in cool, dark place (do not refrigerate).

1. With fingers, strip all stems of remaining leaves. Using garden scissors, cut stems to approximately 6" long.

2. Select dominant flower for center of tussie-mussie (roses shown). Use up to 3 flowers for center. Encircle central flowers with mixed foliage (holly and berries, peppermint, parsley, rosemary, and baby's breath shown). Tightly wrap stems with florist's tape.

3. Add ring of outer flowers (carnations shown). Arrangement should measure approximately 4" in diameter.

4. Frame arrangement with a circle of dark green leaves (ivy shown).

5. Trim stems to approximately 4" long and tightly wrap again with florist's tape. To add extra moisture, wrap wet moss or facial tissue around stems before wrapping with tape.

6. Insert tussie-mussie into lace collar or paper doily with hole cut in center. To make your own lace collar, using elasticized thread, run gathering stitch along 1 edge of 12" length of 3"- to 4"-wide lace. Pull to gather slightly; tack ends together to form circle. Tie ribbon in a bow underneath collar; insert into posy holder if desired.

Glamour Gloves

You will need (for 1 pair of gloves):
pair of cotton knit gloves
5" square piece cardboard
desired trim: 1⅔ yards 2"-wide plaid ribbon for
    red gloves; 19" length 1½"-wide brocade
    ribbon and 20" length ¼" red upholstery
    cording for white gloves; ⅔ yard 4"-wide ecru
    lace for teal gloves
liquid ravel preventer

Note: Seam allowances are ¼". Stretch top edge of glove over cardboard to straighten.

1. For **red gloves**, cut 2 (24") lengths and 1 (12") length from ribbon. Run gathering thread along 1 long edge of each 24" ribbon; gather each to measure 12". With right sides facing and raw edges aligned, stitch ends of each piece together to form a circle.

2. Slip 1 ribbon circle over each glove, aligning seams in ribbons with pinky finger side of gloves. Tack gathered edge of each ribbon to top of cuff.

3. To cover gathered edge of ribbon, cut 12" length of ribbon in half lengthwise. With right sides facing and raw short edges aligned, stitch ends of each piece together to form a circle. With right sides facing and seams aligned, on each glove, stitch raw edge of 1 circle to gathered edge of ribbon. Fold each ribbon over cuff and stitch to inside.

4. For **white gloves**, cut 2 (9½") lengths from brocade ribbon and 2 (10") lengths from cording. With right sides facing and raw edges aligned, stitch ends of each brocade ribbon piece together to form a circle. Stitch 1 brocade circle to each cuff, as in Step 2. Apply ravel preventer to ends of each piece of cording. Leaving ½" free at each end and starting at seam, tack 1 piece to each cuff, covering top edge of ribbons. Tack ends of cording to inside of gloves.

5. For **teal gloves**, cut 2 (12") lengths from lace. Run a gathering thread along top edge of each piece. Pull to gather slightly. With right sides facing and raw edges aligned, stitch ends of each piece together to form a circle. Stitch 1 lace circle to each glove, as in Step 2, attaching each circle to inside of cuff so that lace covers top edge of glove.

CREATIVE WRAPPINGS

Put your seal on a fancy holiday with these clever ideas.

To add a grace note to the simplest of packages, we combined handmade wax seals with art paper, natural materials, and gold leaf. It's a simple matter to customize the idea.

To make the **wax seals**, work on a well-protected surface. Hold 1 end of a wax stick over a flame to melt it. Press the stick onto a sheet of waxed paper and rub in a circular motion to make a thick wax circle. If you use a wax stick that has a wick, allow the melted wax to drip onto the waxed paper, forming a thick wax circle.

Lightly coat the surface of the stamp with mineral oil. Press the stamp into the wax circle and hold for 30 seconds to set the design. Remove the stamp and let the seal dry for a few minutes on the waxed paper. Repeat to make several seals at once. If desired, rub the seals with a bronzing powder to accent the highlights of the design.

Carefully remove the seals from the waxed paper and glue them to the desired packages, gift tags, ribbons, or stationery. For the wax seal-making supplies shown here, see Sources on page 156.

Dad —
Merry
Christmas!
— Frances

Holiday Open House
Christmas Eve 4:00 p.m.
Frances and Phil Willmarth
348 South Wilshire Lane

Todd —
Enjoy!
Love,
Frances

Green-and-Purple
Striped Bag

Purple Velvet Bag

Red Brocade Bag

Plaid Taffeta
Beaded Bag

Great Expectations

Because big treats come in little packages, hopes will be high when they spy these elegant gift bags.

You will need (for each bag):
9" square fabric
desired trims: ribbon, upholstery cording, tassels,
    beads (See Step 3 below.)
liquid ravel preventer

Note: Finished size is 4¼" x 6¾"; adjust fabric size as needed for larger or smaller bag. Seam allowance is ¼". For fabrics and trims, see Sources on page 156.

1. With right sides facing and raw edges aligned, fold fabric in half and stitch along long open edge and 1 short edge. Clip corners and turn.

2. Fold top raw edge 2" to inside of bag.

3. Referring to photo, finish with desired trims as described below. Apply liquid ravel preventer to cut ends of ribbons, threads, and cording.

For **Purple Velvet Bag**, cut 17" length of 1½"-wide gold satin ribbon. Tack 1 (3") tassel to each end of ribbon. Tie ribbon in knot around bag.

For **Green-and-Purple Striped Bag**, cut 17" length of 1½"-wide picot satin ribbon and tie in loose knot around bag. Tack 3" tassel to outer layer of knot.

For **Plaid Taffeta Beaded Bag**, using doubled strand of heavy thread, insert needle up through bottom corner of bag at seam and exit ½" away from seam. Trim thread to 3" tails. Thread 2 to 3 beads on each tail and knot end of thread to secure beads. Trim thread flush with knot. Repeat to make total of 8 strands of beads. Cut 17" length of 1½"-wide green velvet ribbon and tie in knot around bag.

For **Red Brocade Bag**, cut 19" length of ¼"-wide gold metallic upholstery cording. Tack 1 (3") red tassel to each end of cording. Double-tie cording around bag.

Remnant Regalia

These posh wrappers are the perfect finishing touch for your holiday gift plants.

Replace ordinary florist's foil with a sophisticated alternative. Made from leftover wallpaper, these wrappers easily fasten with an adhesive strip. For wallpaper, see Sources on page 156.

You will need:
empty plastic or clay pot (same size as pot for
**   your purchased plant)**
1 sheet white posterboard
spray adhesive
wallpaper scrap (approximately same size as
**   posterboard)**
double-sided tape

Note: Above materials will yield wrappers for 1 (6"-diameter) and 1 (8"-diameter) pot.

1. With a pencil, mark bottom rim of pot, dividing circle into 8 equal sections. Indicate 1 place as a starting point. Place pot on its side on posterboard. Beginning at starting point, mark horizontal lines on posterboard at top and bottom rim of pot. In same manner, roll to next mark on pot and mark horizontal lines. Continue marking until you return to starting point. Connect marks, forming solid, curved lines at top and bottom of pattern. At each end, draw vertical line connecting top and bottom lines. Add 1" overlap to pattern on 1 end. Add ½" along top of pattern for lip so that pot doesn't show when wrapped. If desired, add scallop pattern along top edge.

2. Coat unmarked side of posterboard pattern with spray adhesive and press wallpaper piece onto posterboard. Cut out wrapper along pattern lines.

3. Fit wrapper around pot, overlapping ends and securing with double-sided tape.

Roasted Olives
in Feta
Cheese

LE PRATOLA

Apricot Studded
Brie Cheese

Harvest Cheddar
Cheese

Pepper
Blue
Cheese

GIFTS OF FOOD

It's better to give something you've cooked yourself, and we offer an appetizing assortment for you. Tops on our list are design-it-yourself cheeses—as appealing as they are tasty.

Design-a-Cheese

Wheels and wedges of cheese you've custom-flavored are the kinds of gifts that everybody loves.

Each design-your-own cheese has a cream cheese base to which you add another cheese and various dried fruit, nuts, herbs, spices, and a decorative edible coating. Place each cheese on a cardboard base for easy transporting. For gift baskets, include apples or pears and a bottle of wine, or a loaf of bread, cutting board, and cheese spreader. Enclose a note that says to serve cheese at room temperature.

Pepper Blue

A peppercorn wreath adds a fiery bite to blue cheese. Remove peppercorns before serving if a milder flavor is preferred.

- 2 (8-ounce) packages cream cheese, softened
- ½ pound blue cheese, crumbled and softened
- ½ cup butter or margarine, softened
- 2 tablespoons frozen limeade concentrate, thawed
- 2 tablespoons honey
- ¼ teaspoon ground red pepper
- ¼ teaspoon black pepper
- ¾ cup toasted walnuts, chopped
  Whole or crushed multicolored peppercorns (optional)

Combine first 3 ingredients in a large mixing bowl; beat at high speed of an electric mixer until smooth. Add limeade concentrate, honey, and ground peppers; blend well. Stir in walnuts. Cover and chill at least 1 hour.

Shape mixture into a cheese round. Sprinkle peppercorns over cheese round, creating a wreath design, if desired. Place cheese round on a cardboard circle. Wrap in plastic wrap. Serve with fruit and crackers. **Yield:** 3½ cups.

Harvest Cheddar

- 1 small onion, finely chopped
- 3 cloves garlic, minced
- 1 tablespoon butter or margarine, melted
- 2 (8-ounce) packages cream cheese, softened
- 2 cups (8 ounces) shredded sharp Cheddar cheese
- 1 tablespoon Worcestershire sauce
- 2 teaspoons rubbed sage
- ½ teaspoon ground white pepper
- 1 (2-ounce) jar diced pimiento, well drained
- 12 slices bacon, cooked and crumbled

Cook onion and garlic in butter in a large skillet over medium-high heat until tender; remove from heat and let cool.

Beat cream cheese at medium speed of an electric mixer until smooth. Add Cheddar cheese, Worcestershire sauce, sage, and pepper; blend well. Stir in onion mixture and pimiento. Cover and chill at least 1 hour.

Shape mixture into a cheese round. Roll in crumbled bacon; cut into large wedges and wrap individual wedges in plastic wrap. Serve with fruit and crackers. **Yield:** 3 cups.

Roasted Olives in Feta

- 1 cup pimiento-stuffed olives
- 1 cup pitted ripe olives
- 3 tablespoons commercial Italian salad dressing
- 3 (8-ounce) packages cream cheese, softened
- ½ pound feta cheese, drained and crumbled
- ½ teaspoon hot sauce
  Garnish: additional assorted olives

Combine first 3 ingredients; stir until olives are coated. Spread coated olives on a 15" x 10" x 1" jellyroll pan. Bake at 400° for 25 minutes or until olives are charred. Let cool.

Combine cream cheese, feta cheese, and hot sauce in a large mixing bowl. Beat at medium speed of an electric mixer until smooth. Coarsely chop roasted olives; stir into cheese mixture. Cover and chill at least 1 hour.

Shape mixture into a cheese round. Cut into large wedges. Garnish, if desired. Wrap individual wedges in plastic wrap. Serve with fruit and crackers. **Yield:** 4 cups.

Roasted Olives in Feta

Apricot-Studded Brie

Create a poinsettia-inspired garnish for this sweet cheese using cutouts of dried apricots and figs.

½ cup apricot nectar
¼ cup light rum
¼ cup honey
1 cup diced dried apricots
½ cup diced dried figs
½ cup golden raisins
1 (8-ounce) round Brie
2 (8-ounce) packages cream cheese, softened
1 (2-ounce) package honey-roasted cashews, coarsely chopped
Sifted powdered sugar
Garnishes: additional dried apricot and fig cutouts

Combine first 3 ingredients in a medium saucepan; bring to a boil. Add 1 cup apricots, ½ cup figs, and raisins; stir well and cook 1 minute. Remove from heat. Cover and let stand 30 minutes. Drain and reserve juice. Set fruit aside.

Remove rind from Brie. Cut cheese into cubes.

Combine cream cheese and Brie in a large mixing bowl; beat at medium speed of an electric mixer until smooth. Stir in soaked fruit, cashews, and 1 tablespoon reserved juice.

Soak a triple layer of cheesecloth in remaining reserved juice; squeeze out excess moisture. Line an 8" round cakepan with cheesecloth. Spoon cheese mixture into pan, spreading evenly. Cover and chill overnight.

Remove cheese mixture from pan; discard cheesecloth. Coat surface of cheese with powdered sugar. Garnish, if desired. Wrap in plastic wrap. Serve with gingersnaps. **Yield:** one 8" round.

Coffee Cake Croutons

Java Gestures

These two gifted sweets begin with the bean.

Coffee Cake Croutons

The taste of this easy dessert brings to mind a freshly baked coffee cake. It makes a great late-night snack or breakfast treat.

    1 (10¾-ounce) frozen pound cake, thawed
    ⅔ cup sugar
    ⅓ cup strong brewed coffee
    ¼ cup Kahlúa or other coffee-flavored liqueur
    1 cup toasted pecans, ground
    ¼ cup sugar

Trim crust from pound cake and cut cake into 1" cubes. Combine ⅔ cup sugar and coffee in a small saucepan; bring to a boil over medium heat, stirring frequently. Boil 1 minute. Remove from heat and let cool 1 minute. Stir in Kahlúa. Pour coffee syrup mixture into a small bowl and let cool completely.

Combine pecans and ¼ cup sugar; stir well. Working quickly, dip each cake cube into coffee syrup. Roll each cube in pecan mixture, coating completely. Let cake cubes dry at room temperature on wire racks at least 2 hours. **Yield:** 3 dozen.

Espresso Fudge

Espresso granules have abundant flavor that mellows with hazelnuts and chocolate cookie crumbs. This recipe is so rich you'll want to cut it into tiny squares.

    15 chocolate wafer cookies
    ¼ cup instant espresso granules, divided
    1½ cups sugar
    ½ cup butter or margarine
    1 (5-ounce) can evaporated milk
    8 ounces vanilla-flavored candy coating, chopped
    1 (7-ounce) jar marshmallow cream
    ½ cup chopped hazelnuts
    1 teaspoon vanilla extract

Position knife blade in food processor bowl. Add cookies and 2 tablespoons espresso granules; process until mixture resembles fine crumbs. Set aside.

Line a 13" x 9" x 2" pan with a large sheet of aluminum foil, allowing foil to extend 1" beyond ends of pan. Butter the foil and set aside.

Combine remaining 2 tablespoons espresso granules, sugar, ½ cup butter, and milk in a large saucepan. Cook over low heat until sugar and espresso granules dissolve, stirring occasionally. Bring to a boil over medium heat, stirring constantly. Boil 5 minutes, stirring constantly, until mixture reaches soft ball stage or candy thermometer registers 234°. Remove from heat.

Add candy coating and marshmallow cream, stirring until candy coating melts. Stir in hazelnuts and vanilla. Gently fold in reserved cookie crumb mixture, creating a speckled effect.

Spread mixture into prepared pan. Let cool completely. Carefully lift foil out of pan. Cut fudge into small squares. **Yield:** 2 pounds.

Espresso Fudge

Holiday Elixirs

Spray a cardboard wine cooler carton with several coats of white enamel paint. Allow to dry; then sponge paint with gold paint. Peel labels from wine cooler bottles; sterilize bottles and save the caps. Fill the bottles with December Fruity and Gingered Citrus Cooler. Recap the bottles and deliver in the painted carton with optional instructions for mixing Sangria and Rum-Spiked Cooler.

December Fruity

  4 cups white grape juice
12 whole cloves
  6 (3") sticks cinnamon
  6 whole cardamom pods
  1 (12-ounce) can frozen cranberry juice cocktail
     concentrate, thawed
2⅔ cups water

Combine first 4 ingredients in a large saucepan. Bring to a boil; cover, reduce heat, and simmer 10 minutes. Remove from heat; let cool.

   Strain juice mixture into a pitcher; discard whole spices. Add cranberry juice concentrate and water, stirring well. Chill thoroughly. **Yield:** 2 quarts.

Note: For Sangria, mix equal parts of December Fruity with your favorite dry red wine.

Gingered Citrus Cooler

1 quart apple juice, divided
1 lime, thinly sliced
1 (2.7-ounce) jar crystallized ginger
1 quart pineapple juice
1 quart orange juice

Combine 2 cups apple juice, lime, and ginger in a small saucepan. Bring to a boil; reduce heat and simmer, uncovered, 3 minutes. Remove from heat; cover and let cool.

   Strain juice mixture into a pitcher; discard ginger and lime. Stir in remaining 2 cups apple juice, pineapple juice, and orange juice; chill thoroughly. **Yield:** 3 quarts.

Note: For a Rum-Spiked Cooler, mix 4 parts Gingered Citrus Cooler with 1 part golden rum.

Winter Blooms

The essence of flowers blooms in cakes that are unforgettable gifts and memorable desserts.

For this luscious jellyroll cake dressed with pansies, fashion your own gift tag using a rubber pansy stamp. The recipe for Orange Essence Cakes makes six individual presents. Place each in a small bakery box and tie with raffia. For specialty items, see Sources on page 156.

Lemon Jellyroll with Pansies

Lemon Jellyroll with Pansies

24 edible pansies
5 large eggs, separated
⅓ cup sugar
1 tablespoon plus 1 teaspoon vegetable oil
1 teaspoon lemon extract
⅔ cup sugar
¾ cup sifted cake flour
1¼ teaspoons baking powder
¼ teaspoon salt
2 tablespoons powdered sugar
Lemon-Cream Cheese Filling

Grease bottom of a 15" x 10" x 1" jellyroll pan; line with wax paper. Grease and flour wax paper and sides of pan. Arrange pansies, stems up, in pan.

Beat egg yolks in a large mixing bowl at high speed of an electric mixer 5 minutes or until thick and pale. Gradually add ⅓ cup sugar, beating well. Stir in oil and lemon extract.

Beat egg whites in a large bowl at high speed until foamy. Gradually add ⅔ cup sugar, 1 tablespoon at a time, beating until stiff peaks form and sugar dissolves (2 to 4 minutes). Gently fold beaten whites into egg yolk mixture.

Combine flour, baking powder, and salt; gradually fold into egg yolk mixture. Carefully spoon batter into prepared pan. Bake at 350° for 12 to 14 minutes or until top springs back when touched.

Sift powdered sugar in a 15" x 10" rectangle on a cloth towel. When cake is done, immediately loosen from sides of pan. Turn out onto sugared towel. Peel off wax paper. Turn cake over, pansy side down. Starting at narrow end, roll up cake and towel together; let cool on a wire rack, seam side down. Unroll cake and remove towel. Spread cake with Lemon-Cream Cheese Filling; carefully reroll cake. **Yield:** 8 servings.

Lemon-Cream Cheese Filling
1 (8-ounce) package cream cheese, softened
3 tablespoons butter or margarine, softened
¼ cup plus 2 tablespoons lemon curd

Beat cream cheese and butter at medium speed of an electric mixer until creamy; stir in lemon curd. Chill thoroughly. **Yield:** about 1⅓ cups.

Orange Essence Cakes

½ cup butter, softened
½ cup sugar
⅓ cup honey
2 large eggs
1¼ cups sifted cake flour
½ teaspoon baking powder
⅛ teaspoon salt
⅓ cup freshly squeezed orange juice
⅓ cup finely chopped pecans
1 teaspoon vanilla extract
½ teaspoon grated orange rind
Grand Marnier Syrup
1 cup sifted powdered sugar
2 tablespoons plus 1 teaspoon Grand Marnier or orange juice

Beat butter in a large mixing bowl at medium speed of an electric mixer until creamy. Gradually add ½ cup sugar and honey, beating well. Add eggs, one at a time, beating until blended.

Combine flour, baking powder, and salt; add to butter mixture alternately with orange juice, beginning and ending with flour mixture. Stir in pecans, vanilla, and orange rind. Spoon batter into 6 greased and floured Bundt-lette pans.

Bake at 350° for 25 minutes or until a wooden pick inserted in center comes out clean. Cool in pans 10 minutes. Remove to wire racks; let cool completely.

Return cakes to pans; poke holes in each cake, using a wooden skewer. Slowly pour Grand Marnier Syrup over cakes until all syrup is absorbed. Let stand 30 minutes for cakes to set. Invert cakes onto wire racks.

Combine powdered sugar and 2 tablespoons plus 1 teaspoon Grand Marnier; stir until smooth. Drizzle glaze over cooled cakes. **Yield:** 6 (4") cakes.

Grand Marnier Syrup
½ cup sugar
¼ cup water
¼ cup Grand Marnier or other orange-flavored liqueur

Combine sugar and water in a saucepan; bring to a boil and cook 5 minutes or until syrupy. Remove from heat; let cool to room temperature and stir in Grand Marnier. **Yield:** ½ cup.

Sauce It Up

The ideal gift for a busy friend? Dinner that begins with a flavorful topper.

Spoon these hearty sauces into attractive half-pint jars (see Sources on page 156) and present with a package of pasta or rice. Include instructions for reheating in the microwave.

Black-Eyed Peas and Sweet Peppers

½ cup chopped cooked ham
½ cup chopped onion
1 medium-size sweet red pepper, seeded and cut into very thin strips
1 medium-size green pepper, seeded and cut into very thin strips
2 tablespoons vegetable oil
1 (16-ounce) can whole tomatoes, undrained and coarsely chopped
1 (15.8-ounce) can black-eyed peas, drained
¼ cup water
½ teaspoon dried thyme
¼ teaspoon pepper
¼ teaspoon hot sauce

Cook ham, onion, and pepper strips in hot oil in a large skillet over medium heat, stirring constantly, until tender. Add tomato with liquid and remaining ingredients.

Bring to a boil; reduce heat and simmer, uncovered, 8 minutes, stirring frequently. Remove from heat and let cool.

Spoon mixture into jars. Cover jars with lids and store in refrigerator. Give each jar as a gift with a package of rice. **Yield:** 2 pints.

Note: To serve, remove lid from jar. Microwave, uncovered, at HIGH 1½ to 2 minutes or until thoroughly heated, stirring after 1 minute. Serve over hot cooked rice.

Prosciutto and Parmesan Cream

4 cloves garlic, thinly sliced
2 tablespoons butter or margarine, melted
2 tablespoons olive oil
¼ pound thinly sliced prosciutto, cut into julienne strips
1¼ cups whipping cream
½ cup freshly grated Parmesan cheese
½ cup frozen English peas, thawed
½ teaspoon rubbed sage

Cook garlic in butter and oil in a large skillet over medium heat until golden, stirring constantly. Remove and discard garlic, reserving butter mixture. Add prosciutto to skillet; cook over medium heat, stirring constantly, 2 minutes.

Stir in whipping cream. Bring to a boil over medium heat, stirring constantly. Remove from heat; add Parmesan cheese, peas, and sage, stirring until cheese melts. Let cool.

Spoon mixture into jars; cover jars with lids and store in refrigerator. Give each jar as a gift with a package of pasta. **Yield:** 2 cups.

Note: To serve, remove lid from jar. Microwave, uncovered, at HIGH 2 to 3 minutes or until thoroughly heated, stirring every minute. Serve over hot cooked pasta.

Golden Onion and Spinach Pesto

The thin layer of olive oil that tops the pesto in each jar helps preserve the sauce's bright green color.

 1 (10-ounce) package fresh spinach
 1 (7-ounce) jar oil-packed sun-dried tomatoes, undrained
 4 cloves garlic, sliced
 1 medium onion, thinly sliced
 ⅔ cup olive oil, divided
 1 cup freshly grated Romano cheese
 1 cup walnuts
 ½ teaspoon salt
    Olive oil

Remove stems from spinach; wash leaves thoroughly and pat dry.

Position knife blade in food processor bowl; add half of spinach and process until finely chopped. Add remaining spinach; process until finely chopped.

Drain sun-dried tomatoes, reserving oil. Coarsely chop tomatoes; set aside.

Cook garlic and onion in ¼ cup olive oil in a skillet over medium heat, stirring constantly, until tender and golden. Remove from heat. Add half of onion mixture, cheese, walnuts, and salt to spinach in food processor; cover and process until smooth, stopping once to scrape down sides. Add remaining onion mixture. With processor running, gradually add ¼ cup plus 2 tablespoons olive oil through food chute in a slow steady stream; process until smooth. Stir in sun-dried tomatoes with oil.

Spoon pesto into small glass jars. Cover with a thin layer of additional olive oil. Cover jars with lids and store in refrigerator. Give each jar as a gift with a package of pasta. **Yield:** 3 cups.

Note: To serve, remove lid from jar. Microwave, uncovered, at HIGH 30 seconds to 1 minute or until thoroughly heated, stirring once. Toss 2 tablespoons pesto with 1 cup hot cooked pasta.

Elizabeth Taliaferro, of Birmingham, Alabama, developed the recipes for all of these enticing food gifts. She says her family proves to be her best taste testers.

CHRISTMAS DINNER

One of Savannah's
favorite restaurants,
Elizabeth on 37th,
yields a marvelous menu
for the holiday's most
notable meal.

Christmas Culinary Charm

Chef Elizabeth Terry brings a glorious display of Southern flavor favorites to your Christmas table.

Devoted to classic Southern-style food, Elizabeth recalls her Southern heritage in this marvelous feast. Its familiar flavors of peanuts, pecans, oysters, Vidalia onions, sausage, grits, and Florida citrus are ingredients Southerners have savored for centuries. Elizabeth is partial to the Oyster-Sausage Bundles that begin the festivities. However, she acknowledges that good company is the heart of this menu.

Elizabeth recognizes that nostalgia plays a definite role in the holiday season. "There are certain things in the South that people will always yearn for, particularly 'the bird,'" Elizabeth quips. "In my home growing up, grandfather was always responsible for the bird. The family would make great reference to it."

Her husband Michael, host and wine steward at the restaurant, suggests sipping 1992 Chateau de Tigne Rosé D'anjou throughout the meal and accompanying the chocolate torte with Essensia, an orange Muscat sweet dessert wine.

For Elizabeth, part of the magic of Christmas is seeing how far you can spread joy. She hosts an annual family gathering at the turn-of-the-century mansion/restaurant the Sunday before Christmas. "Above all, Christmas is a celebration time for family, and good food is historically an integral part," she says, smiling.

Menu

Serves 8

Oyster-Sausage Bundles

Cream of Butternut Squash Soup

Orange and Pear Salad with Sesame Dressing

Mustard Spiced Ham or Turkey Roasted with Grape and Peanut Stuffing

Vidalia Onion and Giblet Gravy

Cranberry Sauce

Spoonbread Soufflé

Warm Broccoli and Cauliflower Toss With Blue Cheese Cream

Wine   Water

Rich, Dense Chocolate-Pecan Torte

Pear-Cranberry-Apple Crisp

Dessert Wine   Coffee

Oyster-Sausage Bundles

Prepare and freeze these before the busyness of Christmas Day baking. They can go straight from freezer to oven.

½ **pound ground spicy Italian sausage**
⅓ **cup minced onion**
1 **(10-ounce) container fresh Standard oysters, undrained**
½ **cup (2 ounces) shredded mozzarella cheese**
¼ **cup (1 ounce) shredded sharp Cheddar cheese**
1 **(17¼-ounce) package frozen puff pastry, thawed**

Remove casings from sausage. Cook sausage and onion in a skillet over medium-high heat until sausage is browned and onion is tender, stirring until sausage crumbles. Drain well; return mixture to skillet.

Drain oysters; cut larger oysters in half, if desired. (Reserve liquor for another use, if desired.) Add oysters to sausage mixture, stirring gently. Cook over medium heat 1 to 2 minutes or just until edges of oysters curl; remove from heat and drain well. Let cool; stir in cheeses.

Unfold thawed sheets of pastry onto a lightly floured surface. Cut each sheet into 8 rectangles. Roll each rectangle to a 5" square. Place 2 tablespoons sausage mixture in center of each square. Bring edges of each pastry square together to cover filling and form a bundle. Pinch and twist edges to seal. Cover and freeze at least 1 hour or up to a week.

Place frozen bundles on an ungreased baking sheet. Bake at 400° for 20 to 22 minutes or until golden. Serve immediately. **Yield:** 16 appetizers.

Oyster-Sausage Bundles

Stress-Free Strategy

Up to one week ahead:
• Prepare and freeze unbaked Oyster-Sausage Bundles.

Three days before Christmas:
• Place turkey in refrigerator to thaw, if preparing a frozen bird.

The day before Christmas:
• Prepare torte. Cover and refrigerate overnight.
• Prepare soup; let cool. Cover and refrigerate overnight.
• Prepare gravy (except for pan drippings); let cool. Cover and refrigerate overnight.

Christmas Day, at least three hours before the meal:
• Chop broccoli and cauliflower.
• Prepare and refrigerate unbaked fruit crisp.
• Bake ham or turkey.

One hour before the meal:
• Prepare salad dressing.
• Bake Oyster-Sausage Bundles.
• Reheat soup.
• Reheat gravy; whisk in turkey drippings.
• Prepare and bake Spoonbread Soufflé.
• Prepare broccoli and cauliflower side dish.

Just before the meal:
• Assemble and toss salad.

During the meal:
• Bake fruit crisp.

Cream of Butternut Squash Soup

This velvety blend is so refined that it needs no garnish.

    6 cups chicken broth
    1 large butternut squash, peeled, seeded, and
        chopped (about 2½ pounds)
    2 cups peeled, chopped baking potato
    1 cup chopped Vidalia onion
    1 cup peeled, chopped fresh pear
    1 tablespoon chopped garlic
    1 teaspoon minced fresh ginger
    ¾ cup heavy whipping cream
    ¼ cup freshly squeezed orange juice
    1 tablespoon freshly squeezed lemon juice
    1 teaspoon salt
    1 teaspoon hot chili sauce

Combine first 7 ingredients in a Dutch oven. Bring to a boil; cover, reduce heat, and simmer 40 minutes or until vegetables are tender.

Place half of vegetable mixture in container of an electric blender; cover and process until smooth. Repeat procedure with remaining vegetable mixture. Return pureed mixture to Dutch oven. Add whipping cream and remaining ingredients; cook just until thoroughly heated (do not boil). **Yield:** 3 quarts.

Orange and Pear Salad with Sesame Dressing

Cutting fresh herbs into julienne strips releases their distinctive flavors. Consider serving this refreshing salad course after the entrée.

    ⅓ cup sesame oil
    2 tablespoons minced shallots
    2 tablespoons orange marmalade
    1 tablespoon apple cider vinegar
    1 teaspoon minced garlic
    ½ teaspoon salt
    ½ teaspoon pepper
    1 large bunch watercress
    4 navel oranges, peeled and chopped
    2 ripe pears, peeled, cored, and chopped
    ½ cup minced green onions
    ¼ cup julienne-sliced fresh basil
    ¼ cup julienne-sliced fresh mint

Combine first 7 ingredients in a small bowl; stir with a wire whisk. Let dressing stand at room temperature 30 minutes for flavors to blend.

Remove and discard large stems from watercress. Combine watercress and remaining ingredients; toss gently. Drizzle dressing over salad. Serve immediately. **Yield:** 8 servings.

Mustard Spiced Ham

Bake this glazed ham in a pan lined with aluminum foil to make cleanup easy.

    1 (6-pound) smoked, fully cooked ham half
    ¼ cup Dijon mustard
    ¼ cup firmly packed brown sugar
    1 teaspoon grated orange rind
    ½ teaspoon ground allspice
    ½ teaspoon ground cinnamon
        Garnishes: orange slices, whole cloves

Trim excess fat from ham. Place ham in a roasting pan lined with aluminum foil.

Combine mustard and next 4 ingredients, stirring well. Lightly brush ham with mustard mixture.

Cover and bake at 350° for 1½ hours. Uncover and brush ham with one-third of remaining mustard mixture. Bake, uncovered, 30 to 45 minutes or until a meat thermometer inserted registers 140°, basting with remaining mustard mixture every 10 minutes.

Transfer ham to a serving platter. Garnish, if desired. **Yield:** 12 servings.

Cream of Butternut Squash Soup

Turkey Roasted with Grape and Peanut Stuffing

1½ cups minced onion
1½ cups minced celery heart with leaves
1 teaspoon grated orange rind
½ teaspoon kosher salt
½ teaspoon freshly grated nutmeg
2 tablespoons peanut oil
2 tablespoons butter, melted
1 cup apple juice
1 tablespoon apple cider vinegar
3 cups seedless red grapes, quartered
4 cups cubed whole wheat bread (6 slices)
⅓ cup unsalted peanuts, toasted
¼ cup regular oats, uncooked
¼ cup apple juice
¼ cup butter, melted
1 teaspoon lemon juice
1 (9-pound) turkey
   Salt and pepper
   Garnishes: celery heart leaves, sage leaves,
   red grapes

Cook first 5 ingredients in hot oil and 2 tablespoons butter in a large skillet over medium-high heat, stirring constantly, 3 minutes. Stir in 1 cup apple juice and vinegar; bring to a boil. Remove from heat and let stand 30 minutes. Add grapes, bread, peanuts, and oats; stir well.

Combine ¼ cup apple juice, ¼ cup melted butter, and lemon juice; stir well and set aside for basting turkey.

Remove giblets and neck from turkey; reserve for Vidalia Onion and Giblet Gravy. Rinse turkey thoroughly with cold water; pat dry.

Spoon half of stuffing into neck cavity. Lift wingtips up and over back and tuck under bird. Spoon remaining stuffing into body cavity. Tie ends of legs together with string.

Place turkey on a lightly greased rack in a roasting pan, breast side up. Sprinkle turkey with salt and pepper. Insert meat thermometer into meaty portion of thigh, making sure it does not touch bone.

Place in a 450° oven; reduce heat to 350° and bake 1 hour. Cover loosely with aluminum foil. Bake 1½ additional hours or until meat thermometer registers 180°, basting with apple juice mixture every 15 minutes. Let turkey stand 15 minutes before carving. Transfer to a serving platter. Garnish, if desired. Reserve pan drippings for Vidalia Onion and Giblet Gravy. **Yield:** 8 to 12 servings.

Note: To make Grape and Peanut Dressing, spoon dressing into a lightly greased 9" square pan. Bake, uncovered, at 350° for 50 minutes to 1 hour. (This is a moist dressing. For a drier dressing, decrease 1 cup apple juice to ⅔ cup.)

Vidalia Onion and Giblet Gravy

   Giblets and neck bone from turkey
1 stalk celery, chopped
1 carrot, scraped and chopped
4 black peppercorns
1 whole clove
5 cups chicken broth
4 cups diced Vidalia onion (3 pounds)
¼ cup butter, melted
2 tablespoons peanut oil
¼ cup cornstarch
½ cup heavy whipping cream
   Pan drippings from roasted turkey
   Salt and pepper

Combine first 6 ingredients in a large saucepan. Bring to a boil; cover, reduce heat, and simmer 45 minutes. Pour mixture through a wire-mesh strainer into a bowl; discard celery, carrot, peppercorns, and clove. Remove meat from neck; finely chop neck meat and giblets.

Cook onion in butter and oil in a large Dutch oven over medium-high heat, stirring constantly, until onion is lightly browned and tender.

Sprinkle cornstarch over onion and cook, stirring constantly, 2 minutes. Add strained broth. Cook over medium-high heat, stirring constantly with a wire whisk, until thickened and bubbly. Stir in chopped neck meat and giblets and heavy cream.

Skim fat from reserved pan drippings of roasted turkey; discard fat. Stir pan drippings into gravy. Cook over low heat, stirring constantly, until thoroughly heated. Add salt and pepper to taste. **Yield:** 6 cups.

"The restaurant is a personal experience I feel compelled to share," says Elizabeth, who makes her family's home in the mansion above what she calls her "fancy mom-and-pop" restaurant.

Spoonbread Soufflé

A Southern tradition in many homes, puddinglike spoonbread usually starts with cornmeal and is baked in a casserole. This delicately flavored version features grits.

  6 cups water
1½ cups quick-cooking grits, uncooked
  1 tablespoon minced garlic
  1 teaspoon salt
  ¼ teaspoon freshly grated nutmeg
  ½ cup (2 ounces) shredded sharp Cheddar cheese
  ⅓ cup heavy whipping cream
  2 large eggs, separated
  2 egg whites

Bring water to a boil in a large saucepan. Gradually stir in grits, garlic, salt, and nutmeg; return to a boil. Cover, reduce heat, and cook 10 minutes or until grits are thickened. Stir in cheese and whipping cream. Remove from heat.

Beat egg yolks. Gradually stir about 1 cup of hot grits into yolks; add to remaining hot grits, stirring constantly. Let cool 5 minutes.

Beat 4 egg whites at high speed of an electric mixer until stiff peaks form. Fold beaten egg whites into grits. Pour mixture into an ungreased 2½-quart soufflé dish. Bake at 400° for 30 to 40 minutes or until puffed and golden. Serve immediately. **Yield:** 8 servings.

Warm Broccoli and Cauliflower Toss With Blue Cheese Cream

  4 cups cauliflower flowerets
  4 cups broccoli flowerets
¼ cup half-and-half
  4 ounces blue cheese, crumbled
½ cup mayonnaise
½ cup chopped green onions
¼ cup chopped pecans, toasted

Cook cauliflower in boiling salted water to cover 5 to 6 minutes. Drain well. Repeat procedure for broccoli.

Heat half-and-half in a saucepan over low heat (do not boil). Add blue cheese and cook, stirring constantly with a wire whisk, until cheese melts. Remove from heat. Whisk in mayonnaise.

Transfer cauliflower and broccoli to a serving bowl. Pour blue cheese cream over vegetables; toss gently. Sprinkle with chopped green onions and pecans. **Yield:** 8 servings.

Rich, Dense Chocolate-Pecan Torte

A dollop of unsweetened whipped cream suits this torte that tastes like a buttery toffee bar.

    1 cup pecan pieces
    ⅓ cup firmly packed brown sugar
    2 tablespoons all-purpose flour
    2 tablespoons butter, chilled and cubed
    ¼ teaspoon freshly grated nutmeg
    6 ounces sweet baking chocolate, chopped
    2 ounces unsweetened chocolate, chopped
    ¾ cup plus 3 tablespoons heavy whipping cream
    1 egg yolk, lightly beaten
      Unsweetened whipped cream

Line bottom of an 8" springform pan with wax paper or parchment paper.

Position knife blade in food processor bowl; add first 5 ingredients. Pulse 10 to 12 times or until pecans are finely chopped and mixture is combined. Firmly press mixture into bottom of prepared pan.

Bake at 325° for 14 minutes; cool in pan on a wire rack. Carefully remove sides of springform pan. Invert crust onto a serving plate. Carefully remove bottom of pan and paper. Replace sides of springform pan around crust on plate.

Place chocolates in top of a double boiler; bring water to a boil. Reduce heat to low; cook until chocolate melts. Remove from heat.

Bring whipping cream to a simmer in a saucepan over medium heat (do not boil). Gradually stir about one-fourth of hot cream into egg yolk; add to remaining hot cream, stirring constantly.

Cook over medium heat just until mixture reaches 160°. Gradually whisk cream mixture into melted chocolate, stirring until thick and blended. Pour chocolate over crust in prepared pan. Cover and chill thoroughly.

Run a knife around edge of pan and carefully remove sides of pan. Let torte stand 10 to 15 minutes before serving. Top each serving with whipped cream. **Yield:** 8 servings.

Chef Elizabeth and host-wine steward Michael Terry

Pear-Cranberry-Apple Crisp

Pear-Cranberry-Apple Crisp

Cranberries, pears, and apples merge in this jeweled dessert. Sprinkle cinnamon-sugar over ice cream to top it off.

  1 cup unbleached all-purpose flour
½ cup firmly packed brown sugar
  2 tablespoons regular oats, uncooked
½ teaspoon ground cinnamon
¼ cup plus 2 tablespoons butter, cubed
¾ cup coarsely chopped pecans, toasted
  4 cups peeled, diced pear (2 pounds), divided
¾ cup sugar
  1 (3-ounce) package dried cranberries, chopped
  2 tablespoons cornstarch
  2 tablespoons honey
  2 cups peeled, diced apple (about 1 pound)

Position knife blade in food processor bowl; add first 4 ingredients. Process until oats are coarsely chopped. Add butter and process until mixture is combined. Stir in pecans. Transfer mixture to a small bowl. Cover and chill.

  Combine 1 cup diced pear, ¾ cup sugar, cranberries, cornstarch, and honey in a large saucepan. Cook over medium-high heat until mixture is thickened (about 3 minutes). Remove from heat and stir in remaining 3 cups diced pear and apple. Pour into a greased 2-quart baking dish. Crumble chilled topping over fruit.

  Bake at 375° for 35 minutes or until golden. Let stand 15 minutes before serving. Serve warm with vanilla ice cream and cinnamon-sugar. **Yield:** 8 servings.

Note: For more information on the restaurant, see Sources on page 156.

TREASURY OF RECIPES

Our favorite holiday recipes
from the kitchens of *Southern Living*
are guaranteed to kindle delicious
Christmas memories.

Mocha Polka

Fresh Grapefruit Cake

Broccoli-Carrot Salad

Raisin-Cinnamon Rolls

Favorites from Christmas Past

Here's our blue-ribbon collection of appetizers, entrées, vegetables, and, of course, desserts. Whether you're looking for the casual or the spectacular, you can rely on these time-honored classics.

Appetizers

Ambrosia Spread

Ambrosia takes on a new role in this slightly sweet spread for gingersnaps or breakfast breads.

> 1 (11-ounce) can mandarin oranges, drained
> 1 (8-ounce) container soft cream cheese with pineapple
> ¼ cup flaked coconut, toasted
> ¼ cup slivered almonds, chopped and toasted

Set aside 3 orange segments for garnish. Chop remaining oranges; set aside.

   Combine cream cheese, coconut, and almonds in a medium bowl; stir until blended. Fold in chopped orange. Arrange reserved orange segments on top. Cover and chill. Serve with date-nut bread, banana bread, or gingersnaps. **Yield:** 1⅔ cups.

Cheese Twists

Recast puff pastry sheets into flaky spiral appetizers seasoned with Parmesan cheese and pepper.

> ½ cup grated Parmesan cheese
> ¾ teaspoon seasoned pepper
> ½ teaspoon dried parsley flakes
> ¼ teaspoon garlic powder
> 1 (17¼-ounce) package frozen puff pastry sheets, thawed
> 1 egg white, lightly beaten

Cheese Twists

Combine first 4 ingredients in a small bowl; stir well and set aside.

   Unfold one puff pastry sheet. Brush lightly with egg white. Sprinkle 2 tablespoons cheese mixture evenly over surface of pastry sheet; lightly press cheese mixture into pastry sheet. Turn pastry sheet over and repeat procedure.

Cut pastry sheet in half; cut each half into 9 strips (about 1" wide). Twist each strip into a tight spiral and place on lightly greased baking sheets.

Repeat procedure with remaining pastry sheet, egg white, and cheese mixture. Bake at 350° for 16 to 18 minutes or until golden. **Yield:** 3 dozen.

Pork Tenderloin Appetizer Sandwiches

    1 (3⁄4-pound) pork tenderloin
    1⁄2 cup Burgundy or other dry red wine
    2 tablespoons olive oil
    1 1⁄2 tablespoons Worcestershire sauce
    1 teaspoon dried thyme
    3⁄4 teaspoon onion powder
    1⁄2 teaspoon cumin seeds
    1⁄4 teaspoon pepper
    1⁄8 teaspoon garlic powder
    1⁄8 teaspoon ground cloves
    1⁄4 cup mayonnaise
    1⁄4 cup spicy brown mustard
       Cocktail rolls

Place tenderloin in a heavy-duty, zip-top plastic bag. Combine wine and next 8 ingredients; pour over tenderloin. Seal bag; marinate in refrigerator 8 hours, turning occasionally.

Remove tenderloin from marinade, reserving marinade. Place tenderloin on a rack in a shallow roasting pan. Insert meat thermometer into thickest portion of tenderloin.

Bake at 425° for 30 to 35 minutes or until meat thermometer registers 160°, basting occasionally with marinade. Let meat stand 10 minutes.

Combine mayonnaise and mustard, stirring well. Cut tenderloin into 1⁄4" slices and serve with mayonnaise mixture on cocktail rolls. **Yield:** 8 appetizer servings.

Spicy Nuts

    3 tablespoons vegetable oil
    1 teaspoon Worcestershire sauce
    3⁄4 teaspoon chili powder
    1⁄2 teaspoon garlic salt
    1⁄2 teaspoon ground red pepper
    1 1⁄2 cups dry roasted peanuts
    1 1⁄2 cups cashews or pecans

Combine first 5 ingredients in a large bowl, stirring well. Add peanuts and cashews, stirring well to coat. Spread mixture evenly in a 13" x 9" x 2" pan.

Bake, uncovered, at 300° for 20 minutes, stirring after 10 minutes. Let cool completely. Store in an airtight container up to 2 weeks. **Yield:** 3 cups.

Four-Cheese Pâté

This flavor-packed spread can be made ahead and refrigerated for up to 1 week.

    1 (8-ounce) package cream cheese, softened
    2 tablespoons milk
    2 tablespoons sour cream
    3⁄4 cup chopped pecans, toasted
    2 (8-ounce) packages cream cheese, softened
    1 (4 1⁄2-ounce) package Camembert cheese,
       softened
    1 (4-ounce) package crumbled blue cheese,
       softened
    1 cup (4 ounces) shredded Swiss cheese,
       softened
       Garnish: pecan halves

Line a 9" pieplate or cakepan with plastic wrap; set aside. Combine first 3 ingredients in a mixing bowl; beat at medium speed of an electric mixer until smooth. Spoon mixture into prepared pieplate; spread evenly to edge. Sprinkle with chopped pecans.

Combine 2 packages cream cheese, Camembert cheese (including rind), blue cheese, and Swiss cheese in a medium mixing bowl; beat at medium speed until smooth. Spoon mixture over pecans into pieplate; spread evenly to edge. Cover and chill at least 2 hours. Invert onto serving plate; carefully remove plastic wrap. Garnish, if desired. Serve with apple wedges and pear slices. **Yield:** 4 1⁄2 cups.

Beverages

Coffee-Eggnog Punch

Stir in coffee with commercial eggnog for a smooth holiday punch.

 2 (1-quart) cartons commercial refrigerated
  eggnog
¼ cup firmly packed brown sugar
 2 tablespoons instant coffee granules
¼ teaspoon ground cinnamon
 1 cup brandy
¼ cup Kahlúa or other coffee-flavored liqueur
 1 cup whipping cream
¼ cup sifted powdered sugar
 1 teaspoon vanilla extract
  Ground cinnamon

Combine first 4 ingredients in a large bowl; beat at low speed of an electric mixer until coffee granules dissolve. Stir in brandy and Kahlúa; chill 1 to 2 hours. Pour into a punch bowl.

Combine whipping cream, powdered sugar, and vanilla; beat at high speed until stiff peaks form. Dollop whipped cream onto punch; sprinkle lightly with additional cinnamon. **Yield:** 9½ cups.

Bourbon Punch

Substitute apple cider for the bourbon for a refreshing all-fruit version.

 1 (6-ounce) can frozen lemonade concentrate,
  thawed and undiluted
 1 (6-ounce) can frozen orange juice concentrate,
  thawed and undiluted
 2 cups bourbon
½ cup lemon juice
 1 (2-liter) bottle lemon-lime carbonated
  beverage, chilled
 1 (10-ounce) bottle club soda, chilled

Combine first 4 ingredients; chill. Stir in lemon-lime beverage and club soda just before serving. Serve over crushed ice. **Yield:** 3½ quarts.

Mocha Polka

Mocha Polka

 1 pint chocolate ice cream
 2 cups brewed coffee, chilled
 1 tablespoon light rum (optional)
  Whipped cream
  Ground nutmeg

Combine first 3 ingredients in container of an electric blender; process until smooth. Pour mixture into glasses; top with whipped cream and sprinkle with nutmeg. Serve immediately. **Yield:** 4 cups.

Breads

Glazed Lemon Muffins

1¾ cups all-purpose flour
  1 teaspoon baking powder
¾ teaspoon baking soda
¼ teaspoon salt
¾ cup sugar
  1 tablespoon grated lemon rind
  1 large egg, lightly beaten
  1 (8-ounce) carton lemon yogurt
¼ cup plus 2 tablespoons butter or
    margarine, melted
  1 tablespoon lemon juice
¼ cup sugar
  2 teaspoons grated lemon rind
⅓ cup lemon juice

Combine first 6 ingredients in a large bowl; make a well in center of mixture. Combine egg, yogurt, butter, and 1 tablespoon lemon juice; add to dry ingredients, stirring just until moistened. Spoon batter into greased muffin pans, filling three-fourths full.

Bake at 400° for 18 to 20 minutes or until golden. Cool in pans on a wire rack 5 minutes; remove from pans and place on wire rack. Prick muffins with a wooden pick. Combine ¼ cup sugar, 2 teaspoons lemon rind, and ⅓ cup lemon juice in a saucepan. Cook over medium heat, stirring constantly, until sugar dissolves. Spoon glaze over warm muffins. **Yield:** 16 muffins.

Mini Sour Cream Muffins

  1 cup butter or margarine, softened
  1 (8-ounce) carton sour cream
  2 cups self-rising flour

Combine butter and sour cream; mix at low speed of an electric mixer until smooth. Add flour, stirring just until blended.

Spoon batter into ungreased miniature (1¾") muffin pans, using 1 tablespoon batter per muffin. Bake at 400° for 16 to 18 minutes or until golden. **Yield:** 3 dozen.

Raisin-Cinnamon Rolls

Raisin-Cinnamon Rolls

½ (32-ounce) package frozen bread dough, thawed
¼ cup butter or margarine, melted and divided
½ cup sugar
⅓ cup raisins
  2 tablespoons chopped almonds, toasted
  2 teaspoons ground cinnamon
  1 cup sifted powdered sugar
1½ tablespoons milk

Roll dough into a 14" x 8" rectangle on a lightly floured surface. Brush dough with 2 tablespoons melted butter.

Combine sugar and next 3 ingredients; sprinkle evenly over dough, leaving a ½" border on all sides. Roll up dough jellyroll fashion, starting with long side. Pinch seam to seal (do not seal ends).

Cut roll into 12 slices. Place slices, cut side down, in a lightly greased 9" square pan; brush with remaining 2 tablespoons melted butter. Cover and let rise in a warm place (85°), free from drafts, 1 hour or until doubled in bulk.

Bake at 350° for 20 to 25 minutes or until golden. **Combine** powdered sugar and milk; stir well. Drizzle glaze over warm rolls. **Yield:** 1 dozen.

Entrées

Dijon-Wine Marinated Rib Roast

1 (3- to 4-pound) boneless rib-eye roast
    or rump roast
½ cup Burgundy or other dry red wine
2 tablespoons freshly ground pepper
2 tablespoons olive oil
1 tablespoon Dijon mustard
½ teaspoon salt
⅛ teaspoon dried tarragon
1 clove garlic, crushed

Place roast in a large heavy-duty, zip-top plastic bag. Combine wine and remaining ingredients; pour over roast. Seal bag; marinate in refrigerator 8 hours, turning bag occasionally.

Remove roast from marinade, discarding marinade. Place roast on a rack in a shallow roasting pan. Insert meat thermometer, making sure it does not touch fat.

Bake at 350° for 1 hour and 15 minutes or until meat thermometer registers 145° (medium-rare) or 160° (medium). Let stand 10 minutes before slicing. **Yield:** 8 to 10 servings.

Note: Rib-eye roasts are also packaged as rib roasts.

Holiday Ham Slice with Cinnamon Apple Rings

1 (1"-thick) slice fully cooked ham (about 2
    pounds)
¼ teaspoon hot sauce
3 medium-size red cooking apples
24 whole cloves
2 cups water
1 cup red cinnamon candies
½ cup sugar

Score fat on ham slice. Place ham slice in a lightly greased large shallow dish; brush with hot sauce. Bake at 325° for 25 minutes or until meat thermometer registers 140°. Transfer to a serving platter.

Core apples and cut into ½"-thick rings. Stick cloves into apple rings. Combine water and cinnamon candies in a large skillet; bring to a boil, stirring until candies dissolve.

Add apple rings; reduce heat and simmer 5 minutes or to desired degree of doneness, turning frequently. Remove apple rings from skillet; set aside and keep warm.

Add sugar to skillet, stirring until sugar dissolves. Bring mixture to a boil; boil 10 to 12 minutes or until mixture is reduced to 1½ cups. Add apple rings to skillet, turning to glaze both sides. Transfer cinnamon apple rings to serving platter. Spoon remaining glaze over ham and apple rings. **Yield:** 6 servings.

Ravioli with Creamy Pesto Sauce

Just add a salad to this easy classic for a quick Christmas Eve dinner.

1 cup whipping cream
1 (3-ounce) jar capers, drained
1 (2.82-ounce) jar pesto sauce
2 (9-ounce) packages refrigerated cheese-filled
    ravioli, uncooked
2 tablespoons pine nuts, toasted

Combine first 3 ingredients in a medium saucepan. Cook over low heat until thoroughly heated, stirring frequently (do not boil).

Cook pasta according to package directions in salted water; drain. Toss pasta with whipping cream mixture and sprinkle with pine nuts. Serve immediately. **Yield:** 6 servings.

Salads

Congealed Cherry Salad

1 (16-ounce) can pitted dark sweet cherries, undrained
1 (11-ounce) can mandarin oranges, undrained
1 (8-ounce) can crushed pineapple, undrained
1 (6-ounce) package cherry-flavored gelatin
1 cup cold water
½ cup chopped pecans
Lettuce leaves
Garnish: fresh cherries (optional)

Drain all fruit into a bowl; stir well. Reserve 1½ cups fruit juice mixture; set fruit aside. Bring reserved juice mixture to a boil in a saucepan. Add gelatin and cook, stirring constantly, 2 minutes or until gelatin dissolves. Remove from heat. Stir in cold water. Chill until the consistency of unbeaten egg white.

Fold in fruit and pecans. Pour mixture into a lightly oiled 6-cup mold. Cover and chill until firm. Unmold onto a lettuce-lined serving plate. Garnish, if desired. **Yield:** 8 to 10 servings.

Note: To unmold with ease, run a knife around edge of mold to break the suction. Gently pull salad away from sides of mold using fingers. Wrap mold in a damp, warm dish towel. Place a serving platter on top of mold and invert. Remove mold.

Congealed Cherry Salad

Lemon-Cream Salad

Lemon-Cream Salad

Substitute lime-flavored gelatin and pistachio nuts for a different flavor twist in this creamy salad.

> 1 cup miniature marshmallows
> 1 (10-ounce) bottle lemon-lime carbonated beverage
> 2 (3-ounce) packages cream cheese, cubed
> 1 (6-ounce) package lemon-flavored gelatin
> 1 (20-ounce) can crushed pineapple, undrained
> ¾ cup chopped pecans
> 1 cup whipping cream, whipped
> Red leaf lettuce leaves
> Garnish: lemon rind knots

Combine first 3 ingredients in a large heavy saucepan; cook over medium heat, stirring constantly, until cream cheese and marshmallows melt. Remove from heat.

Add gelatin, stirring until dissolved. Stir in pineapple and pecans. Chill until the consistency of unbeaten egg white.

Fold in whipped cream. Pour mixture into 12 lightly oiled ½-cup molds. Cover and chill until firm. Unmold onto lettuce-lined salad plates. Garnish, if desired. **Yield:** 12 servings.

Artichokes Vinaigrette

> 2 (9-ounce) packages frozen artichoke hearts
> 1 (4-ounce) jar diced pimiento, drained
> ½ cup vegetable oil
> ½ cup white wine vinegar
> 2 tablespoons chopped sweet pickle
> 1 tablespoon dried oregano
> ½ teaspoon dried basil

Cook artichokes according to package directions; drain. Place in a glass bowl. Add pimiento; toss gently.

Combine oil and remaining ingredients in a jar; cover tightly and shake vigorously. Pour over artichokes; toss gently. Chill until ready to serve. Serve with a slotted spoon. **Yield:** 6 servings.

Broccoli-Carrot Salad

1½ pounds fresh broccoli
  1 cup scraped, sliced, or shredded carrot
  1 cup (4 ounces) shredded Cheddar cheese
½ cup mayonnaise
2 to 3 tablespoons sugar
  2 teaspoons red wine vinegar
    Lettuce leaves (optional)
  8 slices bacon, cooked and crumbled

Remove broccoli leaves and cut off tough ends of stalks; discard. Wash broccoli thoroughly and cut into flowerets. Blanch broccoli in boiling water 10 seconds. Plunge into ice water to stop cooking; drain well.

Combine broccoli, carrot, and cheese, tossing gently. Combine mayonnaise, sugar, and vinegar; stir well. Add mayonnaise mixture to broccoli mixture and toss gently.

Spoon broccoli mixture onto lettuce-lined salad plates, if desired, using a slotted spoon. Sprinkle with bacon and serve immediately. **Yield:** 8 servings.

Goat Cheese and Greens

  1 (11-ounce) package goat cheese, cut into 12 rounds
½ cup Italian-seasoned breadcrumbs
    Vegetable cooking spray
⅓ cup olive oil
  3 tablespoons lemon juice
  1 teaspoon dried basil
¼ teaspoon salt
⅛ teaspoon pepper
  1 head radicchio, torn
  2 bunches arugula, torn

Dredge goat cheese slices in breadcrumbs; spray lightly with cooking spray. Place on a lightly greased baking sheet. Bake at 400° for 7 minutes or until golden.

Combine olive oil and next 4 ingredients in a jar. Cover tightly and shake vigorously. Arrange radicchio and arugula on individual salad plates. Top each serving with 2 slices goat cheese; drizzle with dressing. Serve immediately. **Yield:** 6 servings.

Broccoli-Carrot Salad

Side Dishes

Bourbon Sweet Potato Casserole

6 medium-size sweet potatoes (about 3 pounds)
½ cup firmly packed brown sugar
½ cup butter or margarine, melted
⅓ cup orange juice
¼ cup bourbon
½ teaspoon salt
½ teaspoon pumpkin pie spice
1 cup miniature marshmallows

Cook sweet potatoes in boiling water to cover 30 minutes or until tender. Drain. Let cool to touch; peel and mash potatoes.

Combine mashed sweet potato, brown sugar, and next 5 ingredients in a large mixing bowl; beat at medium speed of an electric mixer until smooth. Spoon mixture into a lightly greased 1½-quart casserole.

Bake at 350° for 30 minutes or until thoroughly heated. Sprinkle with marshmallows and bake 5 additional minutes or until marshmallows are golden. **Yield:** 8 to 10 servings.

Deviled Brussels Sprouts

1½ pounds fresh brussels sprouts
⅔ cup butter or margarine, melted
2 tablespoons honey mustard
1 teaspoon Worcestershire sauce
½ teaspoon salt
¼ teaspoon ground red pepper

Wash brussels sprouts thoroughly and remove discolored leaves. Cut off stem ends and slash bottom of each sprout with a shallow X.

Place sprouts in boiling salted water. Cover, reduce heat, and simmer 15 minutes or until tender. Drain well and place in a serving dish.

Combine butter and remaining ingredients; stir well and pour over warm brussels sprouts. Serve hot. **Yield:** 6 servings.

Sausage Dressing

1 pound mild or hot ground pork sausage
4 stalks celery, diced
2 medium onions, diced
5 cups cornbread crumbs
3½ cups chicken or turkey broth
3 cups white bread cubes, toasted
2 teaspoons rubbed sage
¼ teaspoon pepper
2 large eggs, lightly beaten

Cook first 3 ingredients in a large skillet over medium heat until sausage is browned and vegetables are tender, stirring until sausage crumbles. Drain.

Combine sausage mixture, cornbread crumbs, and remaining ingredients, stirring well. Spoon mixture into a greased 13" x 9" x 2" baking dish.

Bake, uncovered, at 350° for 35 to 40 minutes or until lightly browned and thoroughly heated. **Yield:** 8 to 10 servings.

Scalloped Potatoes

1 shallot, minced
1 large clove garlic, minced
½ teaspoon dried crushed red pepper
3 tablespoons butter or margarine, melted
1½ cups whipping cream
1¼ cups milk
½ teaspoon salt
¼ teaspoon freshly ground pepper
2½ pounds red potatoes, unpeeled and cut into ⅛" slices
1 cup (4 ounces) shredded Gruyère cheese
¼ cup freshly grated Parmesan cheese

Cook first 3 ingredients in butter in a Dutch oven over medium heat, stirring constantly, until tender. Add whipping cream and next 3 ingredients; bring to a boil, stirring occasionally. Stir in potato.

Spoon mixture into a lightly greased 2½-quart shallow baking dish; sprinkle with cheeses.

Bake at 350° for 1 hour or until potato is tender. (Cover with aluminum foil the last 10 minutes of baking, if necessary, to prevent excessive browning.) Let stand, covered, 10 minutes. **Yield:** 8 servings.

Desserts

Amaretto-Hot Fruit Compote

1 (17-ounce) can apricot halves
1 (16½-ounce) can pitted dark sweet cherries
1 (16-ounce) can peach halves
1 (16-ounce) can pear halves
1 (15¼-ounce) can pineapple chunks
12 soft coconut macaroons, crumbled
1 (2¼-ounce) package sliced almonds, toasted and divided
¼ cup butter or margarine
⅓ cup amaretto or other almond-flavored liqueur

Drain fruit, reserving syrup for another use.

Combine fruit in a large bowl. Place half of fruit mixture in an 11" x 7" x 1½" baking dish; sprinkle with half of crumbled macaroons. Sprinkle 3 tablespoons almonds over macaroons and dot with 2 tablespoons butter. Repeat procedure using remaining fruit mixture, remaining macaroons, 3 tablespoons almonds, and remaining butter. Drizzle amaretto evenly over fruit mixture.

Bake at 350° for 25 minutes or until bubbly. Sprinkle with remaining almonds before serving. **Yield:** 12 servings.

Caramel-Coconut Pie

¼ cup butter or margarine
1 (7-ounce) package flaked coconut
½ cup chopped pecans
1 (8-ounce) package cream cheese, softened
1 (14-ounce) can sweetened condensed milk
1 (16-ounce) container frozen whipped topping, thawed
2 baked 9" pastry shells
1 (12-ounce) jar caramel ice cream topping
  Garnish: pecan halves

Melt butter in a large skillet. Add coconut and ½ cup pecans; cook until golden, stirring frequently. Set mixture aside and let cool slightly.

Combine cream cheese and sweetened condensed milk; beat at medium speed of an electric mixer until smooth. Fold in whipped topping.

Layer ¼ of cream cheese mixture in each pastry shell. Drizzle ¼ of caramel topping over each pie. Sprinkle ¼ coconut mixture evenly over each pie.

Repeat layers with remaining cream cheese mixture, caramel topping, and coconut mixture. Cover and freeze pies at least 8 hours.

Let frozen pies stand at room temperature 5 minutes before slicing. Garnish, if desired. **Yield:** two 9" pies.

Cheddar-Pear Cobbler

6 medium pears, peeled, cored, and sliced
   (about 7 cups)
1 tablespoon lemon juice
1 cup sugar
3 tablespoons all-purpose flour
½ teaspoon ground cinnamon
½ teaspoon ground nutmeg
   Dash of salt
1 tablespoon butter or margarine
   Cheddar Cheese Pastry

Toss pear slices with lemon juice in a large bowl; add sugar and next 4 ingredients, tossing gently to combine. Spoon pear mixture into a greased 10" x 6" x 2" baking dish; dot with butter.

   Roll Cheddar Cheese Pastry out on a lightly floured surface to a 10" x 6" rectangle; cut lengthwise into ½" strips. Arrange strips in a lattice design over pear mixture; trim excess pastry as needed.

   Bake at 350° for 1 hour or until pastry is golden. **Yield:** 6 to 8 servings.

Cheddar Cheese Pastry
1 cup all-purpose flour
½ teaspoon salt
⅓ cup shortening
¼ cup (1 ounce) shredded sharp Cheddar cheese
2 to 3 tablespoons cold water

Combine flour and salt; cut in shortening with pastry blender until mixture is crumbly. Stir in cheese. Sprinkle cold water (1 tablespoon at a time) evenly over surface; stir with a fork until dry ingredients are moistened. Shape into a ball. **Yield:** pastry for 1 cobbler.

Coconut-Spice Cake

¾ cup butter or margarine, softened
1½ cups sugar
3 large eggs
1 cup buttermilk
½ cup orange juice
2½ cups all-purpose flour
1½ teaspoons baking soda
1 teaspoon salt
1 teaspoon ground cinnamon
½ teaspoon ground allspice
½ teaspoon ground ginger
⅛ teaspoon ground nutmeg
1 cup chopped pecans
2 tablespoons grated orange rind
1 teaspoon orange extract
1 teaspoon vanilla extract
   Seven-Minute Frosting
1 (3½-ounce) can flaked coconut
   Garnish: pecan halves

Beat butter at medium speed of an electric mixer until creamy; gradually add sugar, beating well. Add eggs, one at a time, beating after each addition.

   Combine buttermilk and orange juice. Combine flour and next 6 ingredients; add to butter mixture alternately with buttermilk mixture, beginning and ending with flour mixture. Mix at low speed after each addition until blended. Stir in pecans and next 3 ingredients. Pour batter into 3 greased and floured 9" round cakepans.

   Bake at 350° for 25 to 28 minutes or until a wooden pick inserted in center comes out clean. Cool cake in pans on wire racks 10 minutes; remove layers from pans and let cool completely on wire racks.

   Spread Seven-Minute Frosting between layers and on top and sides of cake. Sprinkle with coconut. Garnish, if desired. **Yield:** one 3-layer cake.

Seven-Minute Frosting
1½ cups sugar
¼ cup plus 2 tablespoons water
1 tablespoon light corn syrup
   Dash of salt
2 egg whites
1 teaspoon vanilla extract

Combine first 5 ingredients in top of a double boiler; beat at low speed 30 seconds or until blended.

Place over boiling water; beat at high speed 7 minutes or until stiff peaks form. Remove from heat; add vanilla and beat 1 to 2 minutes or until frosting is thick enough to spread. Spread immediately on cooled cake. **Yield:** 3½ cups.

Fresh Grapefruit Cake

Freshly squeezed grapefruit juice makes the difference in this light citrus cake.

⅔ cup butter or margarine, softened
1¾ cups sugar
2 large eggs
3 cups sifted cake flour
2½ teaspoons baking powder
½ teaspoon salt
½ cup freshly squeezed grapefruit juice
¾ cup milk
1 teaspoon grated grapefruit rind
1½ teaspoons vanilla extract
   Grapefruit Frosting

Beat butter at medium speed of an electric mixer until creamy; gradually add sugar, beating well. Add eggs, one at a time, beating after each addition.

Combine flour, baking powder, and salt; add to butter mixture alternately with grapefruit juice, beginning and ending with flour mixture. Mix at low speed after each addition until blended. Gradually add milk. Stir in grapefruit rind and vanilla. Pour batter into 2 greased and floured 9" round cakepans.

Bake at 350° for 25 minutes or until a wooden pick inserted in center comes out clean. Cool in pans on wire racks 10 minutes; remove from pans and let cool completely on wire racks.

Spread frosting between layers and on top and sides of cake. **Yield:** one 2-layer cake.

Grapefruit Frosting
1½ cups sugar
2 egg whites
1 tablespoon light corn syrup
⅛ teaspoon salt
⅓ cup freshly squeezed grapefruit juice
1 tablespoon grated grapefruit rind

Fresh Grapefruit Cake

Combine first 5 ingredients in top of a double boiler. Beat at low speed 30 seconds or just until blended.

Place over boiling water; beat at high speed 7 minutes or until stiff peaks form. Remove from heat. Add grapefruit rind; beat 1 to 2 minutes or until frosting is thick enough to spread. Spread immediately on cooled cake. **Yield:** 3½ cups.

Patterns

Starry Night Cut-Ups for the Tree

**Instructions begin on page 46.
Patterns are full size.**

Tree Skirt Cutting Diagram

27"

3"

Cutting lines

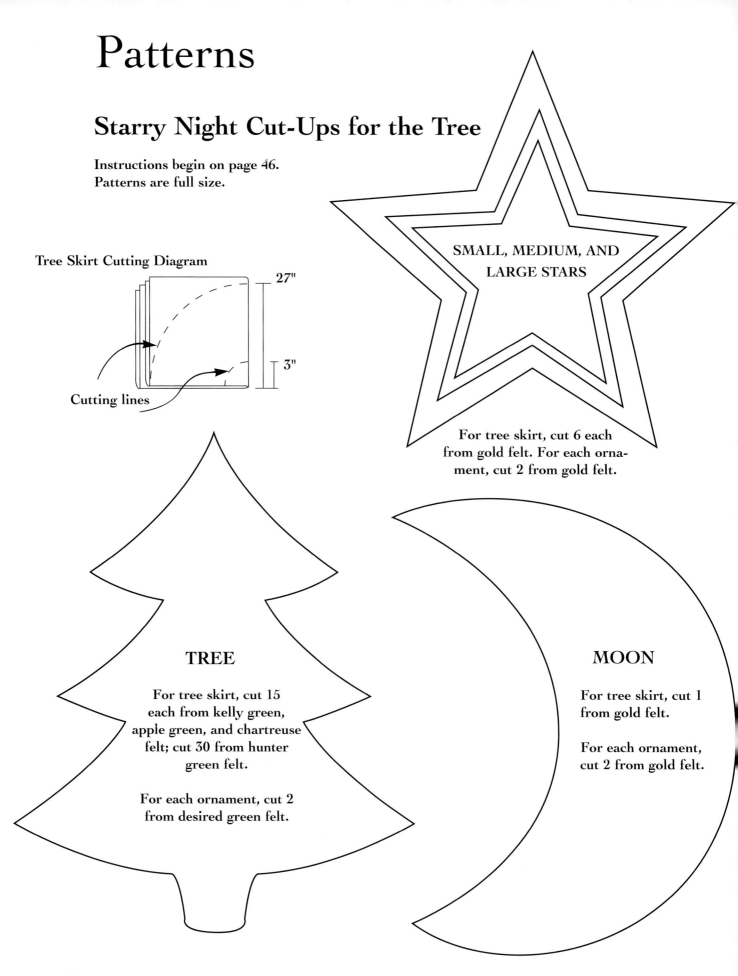

SMALL, MEDIUM, AND
LARGE STARS

For tree skirt, cut 6 each
from gold felt. For each ornament, cut 2 from gold felt.

TREE

For tree skirt, cut 15
each from kelly green,
apple green, and chartreuse
felt; cut 30 from hunter
green felt.

For each ornament, cut 2
from desired green felt.

MOON

For tree skirt, cut 1
from gold felt.

For each ornament,
cut 2 from gold felt.

Toile-la-la Stockings

Instructions begin on page 48.
Patterns include ½" seam allowances.

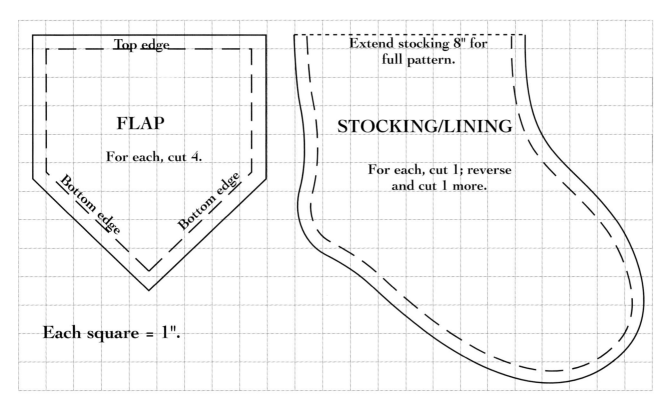

Top edge

FLAP

For each, cut 4.

Bottom edge

Bottom edge

Bottom edge

Each square = 1".

Extend stocking 8" for
full pattern.

STOCKING/LINING

For each, cut 1; reverse
and cut 1 more.

Snowflake Valance and Ornaments

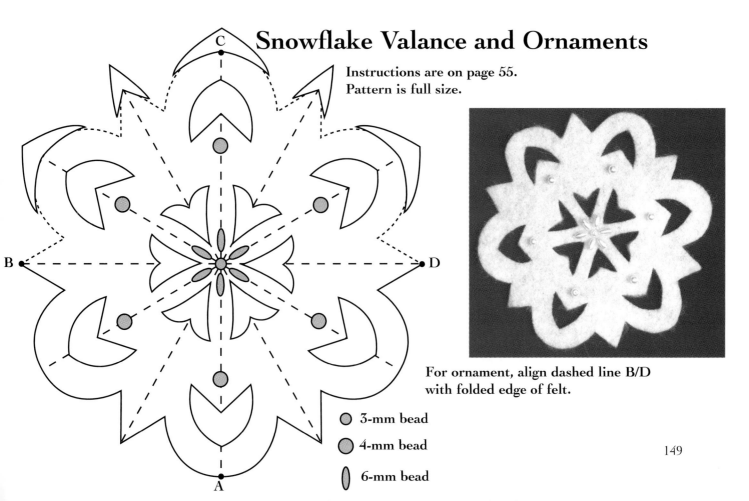

C

Instructions are on page 55.
Pattern is full size.

B

D

For ornament, align dashed line B/D
with folded edge of felt.

🔵 3-mm bead

🔵 4-mm bead

🔵 6-mm bead

A

149

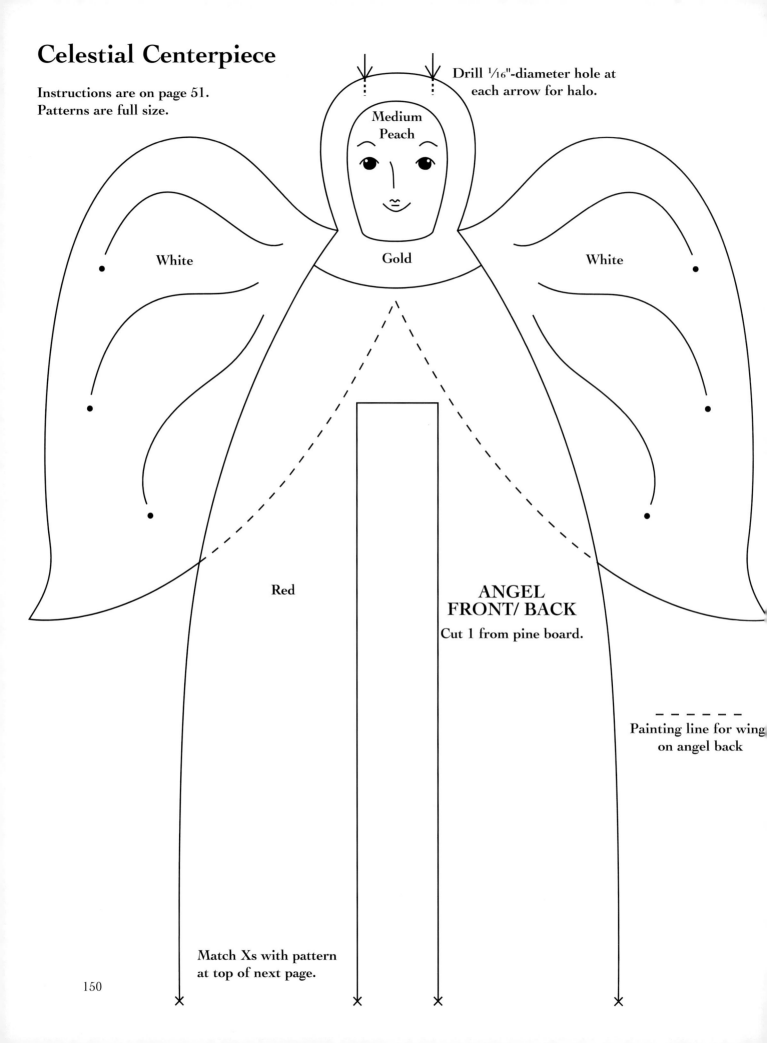

Celestial Centerpiece

Instructions are on page 51.
Patterns are full size.

Drill 1/16"-diameter hole at each arrow for halo.

Medium Peach

White

Gold

White

Red

ANGEL
FRONT/ BACK

Cut 1 from pine board.

Painting line for wing
on angel back

150

Match Xs with pattern
at top of next page.

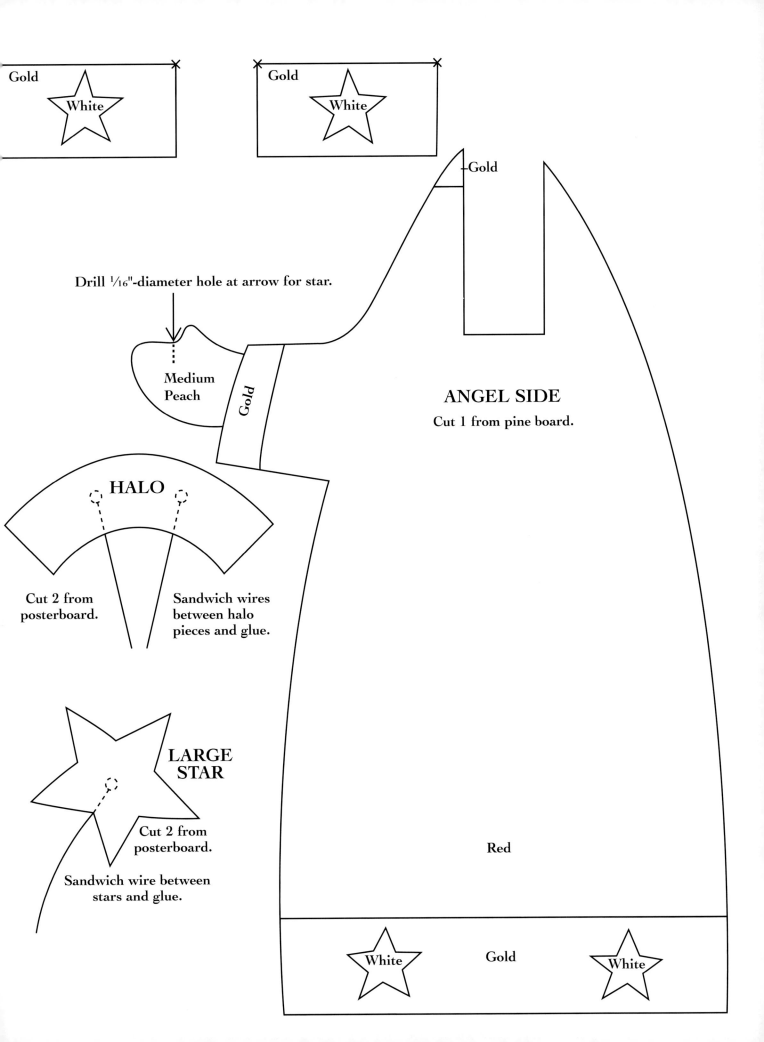

Gold

White

Gold

White

Gold

Drill ¹/₁₆"-diameter hole at arrow for star.

Medium
Peach

Gold

ANGEL SIDE

Cut 1 from pine board.

HALO

Cut 2 from
posterboard.

Sandwich wires
between halo
pieces and glue.

LARGE
STAR

Cut 2 from
posterboard.

Sandwich wire between
stars and glue.

Red

White

Gold

White

A Merry Welcome

Instructions are on page 61.
Pattern is full size.

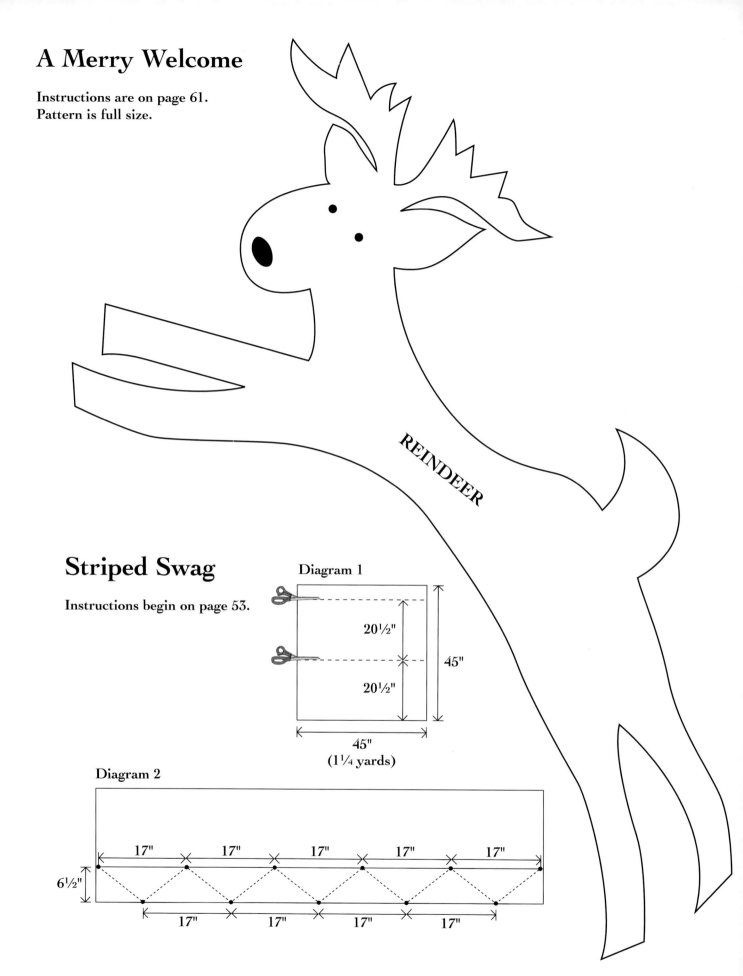

REINDEER

Striped Swag

Instructions begin on page 53.

Diagram 1

20½"

20½"

45"

45"
(1¼ yards)

Diagram 2

17" 17" 17" 17" 17"

6½"

17" 17" 17" 17"

Stencil Magic

Instructions begin on page 63.
Patterns are full size.

SMALL
HOLLY LEAF

LARGE HOLLY
LEAF

LARGE
BERRY

SMALL
BERRIES

Papier-mâché Panache

Instructions begin on page 97.
For star, use desired pattern on page 148.

LEAF

Rose Garland

Instructions are on page 55.

Diagram 1

Diagram 2

Diagram 3

Diagram 4

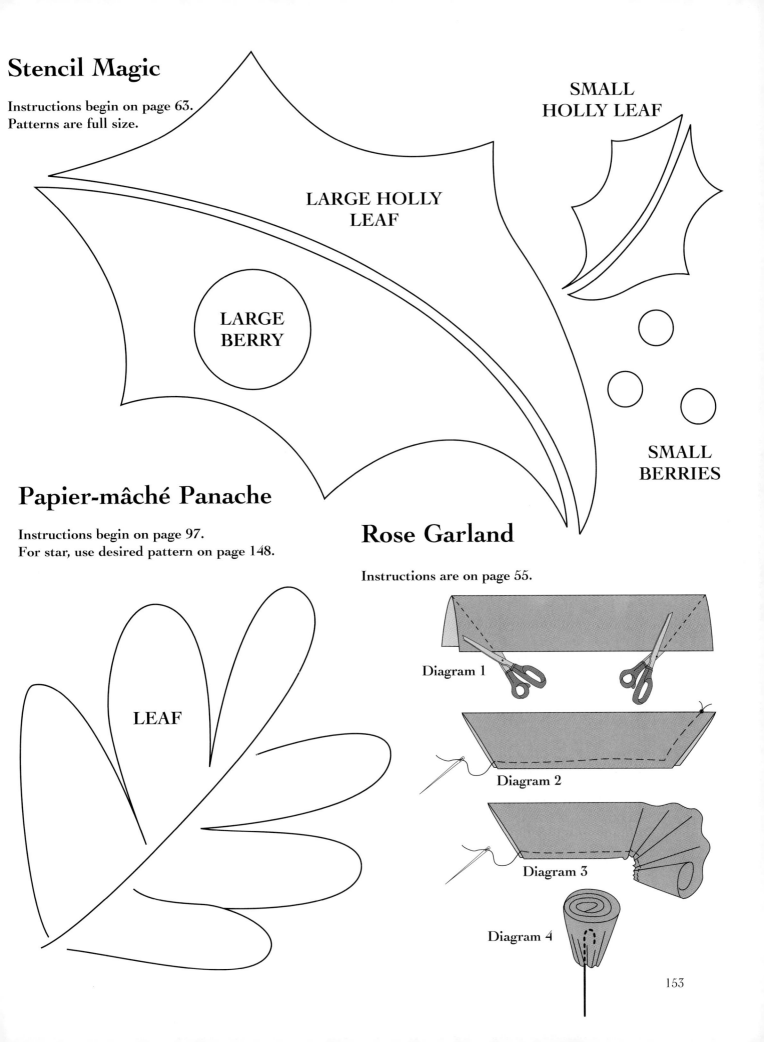

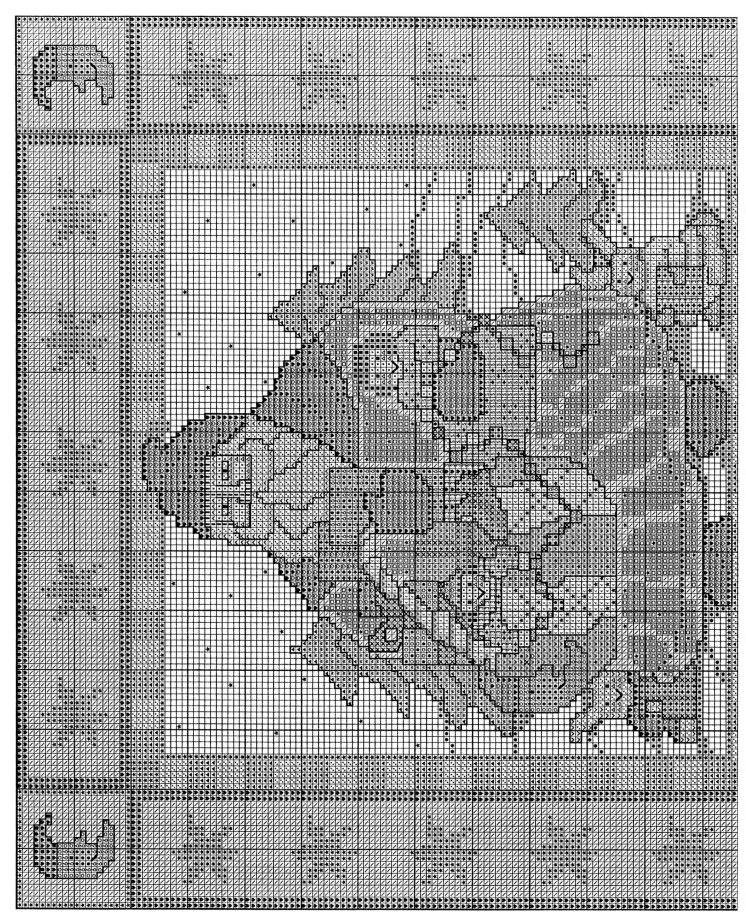

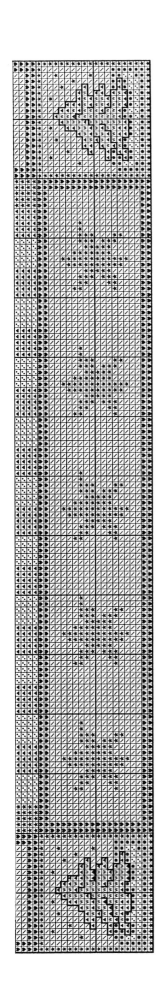

A Jolly Santa to Stitch

Instructions are on page 67.

Note: Numbers are for DMC floss. Blending filament and gold braid are from Kreinik. Cross-stitch over 1 thread, using 2 strands of floss. For snow, use 2 strands each of floss and blending filament. For backstitching, use 1 strand of floss. For stars and borders, use whole gold braid.

Ornaments

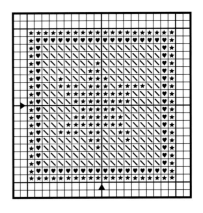

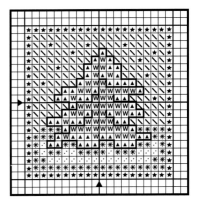

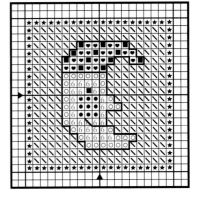

Cross-stitch (2 strands)

DMC		Color Name
White	⋅	White
712	∨	Cream
498	♥	Christmas Red-dk.
321	♡	Christmas Red
820	∖	Royal Blue-vy. dk.
797	⊓	Royal Blue
3761	S	Sky Blue-lt.
3756 032	✳	Baby Blue-ultra vy. lt. + Kreinik Metallic blending filament
3818	▲	Emerald Green-ultra vy. dk.
701	W	Christmas Green-lt.
703	<	Chartreuse
310	■	Black
762	∧	Pearl Gray-vy. lt.
819	▫	Baby Pink-lt.
776	△	Pink-med.
3805	3	Cyclamen Pink
3713	▮	Salmon-vy. lt.
973	○	Canary-bright
972	●	Canary-deep
307	6	Lemon
209	+	Lavender-dk.
996	×	Electric Blue-med.
202HL	★	Aztec Gold Kreinik fine (#8) braid

Backstitch (1 strand)

699		Christmas Green (trees)
310		Black (all else)

Sources

Page 6—ornaments: House of Hatten, 301 Inner Loop Road, Georgetown, TX 78626, or call (800) 542-8836.

Page 9—"Tiffany Holiday" china pattern: Tiffany & Company, 3500 Peachtree Road NE, Phipps Plaza, Atlanta, GA 30326, or call (404) 261-0074.

Page 11—dried and gilded lemon leaves: For information on stores carrying lemon leaves, call The Heeney Company at (404) 351-0000.

Page 12—raffia: Loose Ends, 3824 River Road North, Keizer, OR 97303, or call (800) 390-9979.

greenery tieback: For free catalog, contact Christmas Forest, 445 Beaver Creek Road, Curtis, WA 98538, or call (206) 245-3202.

paperwhite bulbs: White Flower Farms, Route 63, Litchfield, CT 06759, or call (203) 496-9600.

ribbon: For information on stores carrying Midori ribbon, call (800) 659-3049.

Page 14—Styrofoam cone: Schrock's International, P.O. Box 238, 110 Water Street, Bolivar, OH 44612. Send $3 for catalog or call (216) 874-3700.

Page 22—pesticide-free flowers: Elegance Distributing Inc., 5480 Bellevue Highway, P.O. Box 275, Eaton Rapids, MI 48822, or call (800) 487-6157.

Page 31—gingham ribbon: For information on stores carrying French Accents ribbon, call (310) 212-3374.

beeswax candles: Primavera, 2655-C Decatur Road, Suite 156, Decatur, GA 30033, or call (404) 373-3914.

Page 34—glass gems: Hill Street Warehouse, 2050 Hills Avenue, Atlanta, GA 30318, or call (404) 352-5001.

votive candle holders: Williams-Sonoma, 100 North Point St., San Francisco, CA 94123, or call (415) 616-8647.

votive candles: Pottery Barn, 100 North Point St., San Francisco, CA 94123, or call (415) 616-8647.

silicone: For information on stores carrying Creatively Yours™ or Duro™ clear silicone, call (800) 562-0560.

Page 38—paperwhite and lily bulbs: White Flower Farms, Route 63, Litchfield, CT 06759, or call (203) 496-9600.

fresh evergreen wreath: Laurel Springs Christmas Tree Farm, P.O. Box 85, Highway 18 South, Laurel Springs, NC 28644-0085, or call (800) 851-2345.

Page 40—dried hydrangea blooms: Green Valley Growers, 10450 Cherry Ridge Road, Sebastopol, CA 95472, or call (707) 823-5583.

Page 43—Styrofoam star, pepperberries, and tallow berries: Craftex Wholesale Distributors, 7215 Ashcroft, Houston, TX 77081, or call (800) 397-1270.

Page 46—felt tree skirt and sheets: Look for Kunin Felt Classic Rainbow™ Felt products at local retail fabric stores, or call (603) 929-6100 for mail order prices.

Page 48—toile and check fabrics: Waverly, 79 Madison Avenue, New York, NY 10016, or call (800) 423-5881.

Page 51—acrylic paints: Look for DecoArt™ paints at local crafts stores. Or contact DecoArt, P.O. Box 360, Stanford, KY 40484, or call (606) 365-3193.

dimensional paints: Look for Tulip paints at crafts stores, or call (800) 458-7010.

Page 53—striped fabric: Schumacher & Company, 79 Madison Avenue, New York, NY 10016, or call (800) 332-3384.

Page 55—felt: Look for Kunin Felt Classic Rainbow™ Felt products at local retail fabric stores, or call (603) 929-6100 for mail order prices.

Page 67—embroidery floss: Look for DMC floss at local needlework and crafts stores. Or contact Craft Gallery, P.O. Box 145, Swampscott, MA 01907, or call (508) 744-2334.

gold braid: Kreinik Manufacturing Company, Inc., 9199 Reisterstown Road, Suite 209B, Owings Mills, MD 21117, or call (800) 537-2166.

Aida cloth: Zweigart Fabrics and Canvas, 2 Riverview Drive, Somerset, NJ 08873-1139, or call (908) 271-1949.

perforated paper: For free catalog send SASE to Yarn Tree, P.O. Box 724, Ames, IA 50010, or call (515) 232-3121.

Page 68—Styrofoam shapes: Schrock's International, P.O. Box 238, 110 Water Street, Bolivar, OH 44612. Send $3 for catalog or call (216) 874-3700.

crinkle wire: D. Blumchen & Company, Inc., P.O. Box 1210-OX, Ridgewood, NJ 07451-1210, or call (201) 652-5595.

dried flowers: Meadow Everlastings, 16464 Shabbona Road, Malta, IL 60150. Send $2 for catalog or call (815) 825-2539.

dried mini rosebuds: Val's Naturals, P.O. Box 832, Kathleen, FL 33849, or call (813) 858-8991.

freeze-dried flowers: Everlasting Gardens, 5445 Oceanus Drive, Suite 112, Huntington Beach, CA 92649, or call (714) 890-7077.

Page 93—polar fleece: Frostline Kits, 2525 River Road, Grand Junction, CO 81505, or call (800) 548-7872.

Page 98—handmade paper: Loose Ends, 3824 River Road North, Keizer, OR 97303, or call (800) 390-9979.

gold-leaf kit: Houston Art & Frame, Inc., P.O. Box 56146, Houston, TX 77256, or call (713) 868-2505.

Page 104—dried flowers and herbs: Meadow Everlastings, 16464 Shabbona Road, Malta, IL 60150, or call (815) 825-2539.

antique posy holders: Twenty-four Karat Antiques, 5360 Peachtree Industrial Boulevard, Suite 10, Atlanta, GA 30341, or call (404) 952-3909.

Page 105—For a copy of Geraldine Laufer's *Tussie-Mussies: The Victorian Art of Expressing Yourself in the Language of Flowers*, contact Frog Holler, 915 Lake Charles Drive, Roswell, GA 30075-3225.

Page 108—wax seal kit: The French Corner, 7 Westchester Plaza, Elmsford, NY 10523, or call (800) 421-7367.

wax sticks with wicks: Victorian Papers, P.O. Box 411342, Kansas City, MO 64141-1341, or call (800) 800-6647.

velvet/satin ribbon: For information on stores carrying Midori ribbon, call (800) 659-3049.

handmade paper: Loose Ends, 3824 River Road North, Keizer, OR 97303, or call (800) 390-9979.

Page 111—fabrics: New York Elegant Fabric, Inc., 240 West 40th Street, New York, NY 10018, or call (212) 302-4980.

beads: The Beadery® Craft Products, P.O. Box 178, Hope Valley, RI 02832.

Page 112—wallpaper: Osborne & Little, Suite 520, 979 Third Avenue, New York, NY 10022, or call (212) 751-3333.

General Index

Recipe Index

Contributors

Designers

Peggy Barnhart, tabletop garland, 32–33; hydrangea garland and wreath, 40–41.
Lula Chang, Woolly Dreams Design, cross-stitched Santa and ornaments, 66–67.
Judy Ford, tassels, 56–59.
Marguerite Jay Gignoux, collage cards, 94–95.
Charlotte Hagood, rose garland, snowflake valance and ornament, 54–55.
Linda Hendrickson, welcome mat, 60–61.
Margot Hotchkiss, tree skirt and ornaments, 44–47; stencil projects, 62–65; floral ornaments, 68–69; gloves, 106–107; gift bags, 110–111.
Heidi Tyline King, gem glassware, 34–35; stockings, 48–49; papier-mâché bowls, 96–99.
Geraldine A. Laufer, tussiemussies, 102–105.
Leigh Pate, striped swag, 52–53.
Lyman Ratcliffe, tree toppers, 2, 37, 42–43.
Carol Richard, topiary trees, 36–37; bulb wreath, 38–39.
Betsy Cooper Scott, wallpaper wrappers, 112–113.
Elizabeth Taliaferro, recipes, 114–123.
Elizabeth Terry, recipes, 124–133.
Dee Dee Triplett, angel, 50–51.
Cynthia Moody Wheeler, blanket and pillow, 90–93.
Nancy Worrell, handkerchief sachet, 100–101.

Photographers

Ralph Anderson, 40–41.
Jim Bathie, front cover; 16–18, 20–21, 23–31, 70–83, 85, 87–89, 114–120, 122–129, 131–136, 138–139, 141–143, 145, 147, 158.
Langdon Clay, 56–59.
Cheryl Dalton, 102, 104–105.
Rick Dean, 39, 44, 46–47, 60, 91.
Chris Little, 7, bottom right; 8, 13, bottom right; 65, top.
Hal Lott, 2, 37, 42–43.
John O'Hagan, front flap; back cover; 3, 5, 6, 9–12, 13, top and bottom left; 14–15, 32–36, 49–50, 52, 54, 62–64, 65, bottom; 66–69, 92, 94–101, 103, 107–113, 149, 155, 157.

Photo Stylists

Kay Clarke, front cover; 16–18, 20–21, 23–27, 28–31, 70–83, 85, 87–89, 114–120, 122–129, 131–136, 138–139, 141–143, 145, 147, 158.
Joetta Moulden, 2, 37, 42–43.
Katie Stoddard, front flap; back cover; 3, 5, 6, 9–12, 13, top and bottom left; 14–15, 32–36, 49–50, 52, 54, 62–64, 65, bottom; 66–69, 92, 94–101, 103, 107–113, 149, 155, 157.

Special Thanks

Thanks to the following talented people:
Julie Azar
Carol Damsky
Rickman Freeman
Alyce Head
Brenda Kujawski
Rita Yerby

Thanks to the following homeowners in Alabama:
Peggy and James Barnhart
Beth and Perry Cook
Celia and Marshall McGarity
Kit Samford
Judy and Hal Sargent
Cameron and Scott Vowell

Thanks to the following businesses:
Bridges Antiques,
Birmingham, Alabama
Bromberg's,
Birmingham, Alabama
Frankie Engel Antiques,
Birmingham, Alabama
Mariposa,
Manchester, Massachusetts
Mesa International,
Elkins, New Hampshire

CHRISTMAS CARD LIST

Name & Address   **Name & Address**